INTENSIVE DICTATION & TRANSCRIPTION

Book 2 C21 Collegiate Series

CENTURY 21 SHORTHAND

IROL WHITMORE BALSLEY, Ed.D.
Professor of Education
Texas Tech University

ROBERT E. HOSKINSON, Ph.D.
Professor of Office Administration
Washington State University

System Design and Research Consultant
EDWARD L. CHRISTENSEN, Ph.D.

Shorthand Plates Written by **STANFORD D. DeMILLE**

Published by
R71 SOUTH-WESTERN PUBLISHING CO.

CINCINNATI WEST CHICAGO, ILL. DALLAS PELHAM MANOR, N.Y.
PALO ALTO, CALIF. BRIGHTON, ENGLAND

Copyright© 1974
By
South-Western Publishing Co.
Cincinnati, Ohio
All Rights Reserved

The text of this publication, or any part thereof, may
not be reproduced or transmitted in any form or any
means, electronic or mechanical, including photocopy-
ing, recording, storage in an information retrieval system, or otherwise, without the prior written permission of the publisher.

ISBN: 0-538-18710-7

Library of Congress Catalog Number: 73-75257

1 2 3 4 5 6 7 H 9 8 7 6 5 4

Printed in the United States of America

Dictionary excerpts found on pages 37 and 38 are taken from
THORNDIKE-BARNHART ADVANCED DICTIONARY, 1973,
and are provided by Scott, Foresman and Company, Glenview, Illinois.

PREFACE

A new approach to the teaching of shorthand/transcription makes this volume unique. Shorthand is presented as a tool of communication in the office, which is, after all, the decision-making center of a business or professional activity.

Concurrent with skill development is the acquisition of knowledge of basic office procedures. An awareness of the secretary's role in expediting executive decisions is created through 30 narrations on such vital topics as sensitivity to time, to maximizing productivity, and to the cost of an error. Thus the skill in using this tool of communication is placed in perspective, enabling the student to enter the business world with a helpful overview of the office function.

Many students work part time or even full time in offices while acquiring their formal education. Therefore, they need basic office procedures information early in their educational program. All too often secretarial-bound students learn these fundamentals the hard way—through sad experience—because their skills courses preceded their office procedures courses.

If the shorthand/transcription program is merely a succession of dictation-transcription—dictation-transcription ad infinitum, the excitement of using this tool of communication is never generated. In this volume, the background of each communication is given before dictation. Thus the reason for creating the memo or letter is known. Opportunities are presented to discuss the nature of the communication and the effectiveness with which it achieves its purpose. Students and teachers alike have the opportunity to relate their on-the-job experiences. Fundamentals of good written communication are injected into the class sessions, lifting the learning out of the monotonous form so often characteristic of the shorthand class that is limited to skill-building *per se.*

Volume I of CENTURY 21 SHORTHAND, Collegiate Series, gave primary emphasis to the learning of the theory of the system, to development of a substantial degree of automatization of the shorthand vocabulary for the 1,500 most-used words in business, and to acquaintanceship with a shorthand vocabulary for more than 4,000 additional words. Considerable pretranscription skill was developed through reviews of English usage in such areas as punctuation, word differentiation, and spelling.

In this volume, approximately one half of the lessons contain information about office procedures and behavior. Each of the lessons also provides material for building skill in note taking and/or transcribing. By the end of Lesson 40, the shorthand outline for each word in the first 3,500 most-used word list has been used at least once. By the end of the final project, each of the 1,500 most commonly used words in business has been used at least twice. Each of the 5,000 most commonly used words has been used at least once.

The performance of the college-educated secretary differs markedly from that of the high school graduate, as it should. She or he understands business operations and sees functional relationships as a result of study in such areas as accounting, finance, marketing, management, and statistics. This person's vocabulary is more likely to be on a par with that of the executive, since the executive is probably a person with collegiate education. The secretary-in-training who uses this book will become acquainted with semitechnical vocabulary in different fields of business and the professions. Because of study beyond high school, the college-trained secretary is more likely to have the breadth of view so essential to being an administrative assistant.

Transcription is recognized in this volume as a complex skill requiring multisensory integration. Students must be *taught*—not just *monitored.* The lessons are carefully organized in accordance with accepted principles of learning a multifaceted skill, moving from the simple to the complex.

The executive secretary can use this tool of communication, shorthand, in ways not open to the machine shorthand writer or the dictation machine operator because of its "portability." It is truly a unique tool for the executive secretary because it is always with the secretary in any situation.

Irol W. Balsley
Robert E. Hoskinson

CONTENTS

UNIT 1 THEORY REVIEW

Lesson	Page
1	2
2	5
3	8
4	12
5	15
6	19
7	22
8	25
9	28
10	33

UNIT 2 COMMUNICATION IN EDUCATION

Lesson	Page
11	36
12	39
13	42
14	45
15	48

UNIT 3 COMMUNICATION IN MANUFACTURING

Lesson	Page
16	51
17	54
18	57
19	60
20	64

UNIT 4 COMMUNICATION IN PSYCHOLOGY

Lesson	Page
21	66
22	69
23	72
24	75
25	79

UNIT 5 COMMUNICATION IN PRINTING AND PUBLISHING

Lesson	Page
26	82
27	85
28	88
29	90
30	94

UNIT 6 COMMUNICATION IN INSURANCE

Lesson	Page
31	97
32	99
33	102
34	105
35	107

UNIT 7 COMMUNICATION IN LAW

Lesson	Page
36	109
37	112
38	116
39	118
40	122

UNIT 8 COMMUNICATION IN ENTERTAINMENT & RECREATION

Lesson	Page
41	126
42	128
43	131
44	134
45	137

UNIT 9 COMMUNICATION IN MEDICINE

Lesson	Page
46	140
47	144
48	147
49	150
50	153

UNIT 10 COMMUNICATION IN TRANSPORTATION

Lesson	Page
51	157
52	161
53	165
54	168
55	171

UNIT 11 COMMUNICATION IN MASS MEDIA

Lesson	Page
56	175
57	179
58	182
59	186
60	190

UNIT 12 COMMUNICATION IN PUBLIC ADMINISTRATION

Lesson	Page
61	193
62	196
63	200
64	203
65	206

UNIT 13 COMMUNICATION IN BANKING

Lesson	Page
66	210
67	212
68	215
69	218
70	223

PROJECT 1 225

PROJECT 2 227

APPENDIX .... I-VIII

The office is the decision-making center of the firm or profession. The executive secretary must, therefore, have much more than a routine skill with tools of communication. She must understand business operations and office procedures if she is to use those tools in a practical and effective way for recording decisions and disseminating them properly. Therefore, the lessons in this textbook are so constructed that knowledge of office procedures is developed concurrently with skill in using shorthand as a communication tool.

An employee who has shorthand skill but who does not understand office operations will be a "robot" worker. She will make foolish mistakes because she does not understand the significance of papers flowing across her desk. She will be unable to make correct decisions about priorities, ethics, or interpersonal matters.

Many secretaries-in-training work part-time as they pursue their studies. There is much information they need to perform even those duties assigned a part-time employee.

In the preceding term you acquired a knowledge of the theory of Century 21 shorthand and developed skill in using the basic shorthand vocabulary for the first 1,500 most-used words. You also gained an acquaintanceship with shorthand outlines for more than 4,000 other words. The secretary must have a vocabulary comparable to that of the executive for whom she works. She is expected to be a specialist in the use of the English language; that is one of her unique contributions to proper communications in the office. By the end of Lesson 40 you will have used at least once every word in the first 3,500 most-used word list. By the end of Lesson 80, you will have used at least once every word in the first 5,000 most-used word list. You will have written shorthand outlines for several thousand other words also.

In the preceding term you also reviewed basic rules of English usage, increasing your skill in punctuating properly, spelling correctly, and selecting the appropriate word for clarity and accuracy of communications.

In the first ten lessons of this volume you will review the Century 21 theory and bring to a higher level of automatization your skill with the basic shorthand vocabulary of business and professional communications.

After Lesson 10, an expansion of your general vocabulary is ensured through a five-lesson concentration on communications characteristic of a certain business or professional field. These fields are: education, manufacturing, psychology, printing and publishing, insurance, and law. In the last half of this volume, you will become familiar with typical communications in other fields.

You will begin the fascinating art of transcription with Lesson 12. Attention is given to the development of this skill in two of every five lessons. The other three lessons are devoted to skillbuilding in notetaking and to office procedures.

The transcription lessons build skill in handling both typing and nontyping aspects of the skill. Mailability is your goal throughout because only usable transcripts are acceptable in the business or professional world. The lessons proceed from the simple to the more complex through carefully controlled instructional material.

Addresses

Mr. Carter prefers that you ask any necessary questions about a piece of correspondence immediately after he dictates it; however, you do not bother him unnecessarily for the spelling of names or for addresses. You usually get such information from your files or from incoming correspondence. Since you will not have access to such sources in this project, you may verify the spelling of names and get addresses from the following list:

Adams, Nancy J. (Miss)
6609 Delmar Road
Indianapolis, IN 46220

Asmus, Nancy T. (Miss)
Editor
Employment Trends
2101 Butler Building
162 North State Street
Chicago, IL 60601

Bell, George F.
Instructor
Plainfield High School
Plainfield, IN 46168

Benner, Mabel C. (Miss)
Counselor
Brazil High School
Brazil, IN 47834

The Daily Star
307 North Pennsylvania Street
Indianapolis, IN 46206

Financial Security, Inc.
134 East Market Street
Indianapolis, IN 46204

Freeman, Bernard F.
Department of Social Welfare
State Capitol Complex
East Sixth and Des Moines Streets
Des Moines, IA 50319

Jacinto, Jose C.
1911 Stewart Avenue
Indianapolis, IN 46220

Ketrow, S. S.
University Accounting Service
1800 University Avenue, West
St. Paul, MN 55104

Lewis, L. K.
1533 Oak Lane
Indianapolis, IN 46220

Richardson, Thomas J.
1421 Priscilla Avenue
Indianapolis, IN 46219

Stockton, Mabel R. (Mrs.)
Council on the Aging
320 North Meridian Street
Indianapolis, IN 46204

Stover, Ellen (Mrs.)
21064 Brewster Road
Indianapolis, IN 46260

LESSON 1

1-A. System Command

How high can you build your speed on the following notes? In the 20 standard words there are 5 phrases and 15 Speedforms or derivatives.

1-B. System Review

This exercise is designed to strengthen your command of the Century 21 system. The principles receiving special emphasis are given with several illustrations. Practice these outlines and then build speed of recall on the continuity material.

fr

ch

-scribe

-ly

-ity

-ble

-ingly

1-C. Recording Fidelity

In any shorthand symbol system several strokes differ from each other only in size or in type of stroke, i.e., straight or curved line. To develop recording fidelity, the writer must strive to maintain proper proportion in his strokes so that reading for transcription is easy and accurate.

The following material contains some outlines that could be misread if they were written in poor proportion. Practice writing the sentences, making a special effort to make each one easily distinguishable.

UNIT 1 THEORY REVIEW

PROJECT 2

EMPLOYER

In this project you will serve as secretary to Mr. Paul L. Carter, president of the CARTER EMPLOYMENT SERVICE. This private employment agency is located at 2802 North Meridian Street in Indianapolis, Indiana. (Telephone: 335-4459)

STAFF

The following individuals comprise the professional staff in the firm:

Phyllis Arnold, Counselor, Office Occupations
H. T. Hendrickson, Counselor, Professional Business Occupations
Lawrence Johnson, Counselor, Skilled Occupations
J. T. Spencer, Counselor, Industrial Occupations
Joyce Taylor, Counselor, Domestic Occupations
Jack S. Teldon, Accountant and Office Manager
William W. Wells, Counselor, Agricultural Occupations

In addition to you, there are two stenographers and two clerk-typists.

DUTIES

While you are primarily responsible for assisting Mr. Carter, you also help members of the staff with their work when the other members of the office force are busy.

Mr. Carter is currently serving as president of the Indiana Private Employment Agency Association. You frequently assist him with work in connection with this organization.

EQUIPMENT

The office force has access to the following equipment: electric typewriters, copying machine, spirit and stencil duplicators, automatic collator, and an electronic stencil maker.

CORRESPONDENCE

The CARTER EMPLOYMENT SERVICE uses 8½ x 11 stationery. The letterhead contains the agency's name, address, and telephone number. The firm uses No. 6¾ and No. 10 envelopes, with printed return addresses.

Whenever the name CARTER EMPLOYMENT SERVICE appears in typewritten copy, it is typed in all capital letters.

All members of the firm use the modified block letter style with blocked paragraphs. They also use mixed punctuation. No subject line is used in firm letters. "Sincerely" is used as the standard complimentary close. The firm name is not typed in the closing lines. Only the typist's initials, in lower case, are used as reference initials.

Interdepartmental correspondence is typed in memorandum form on plain bond paper. Members of the staff use Style 2 that is illustrated on page i of the Appendix. Because this is a small firm, no titles are used after the names in the *To* and *From* sections. The typist is expected to provide an appropriate subject line for each memorandum.

Mr. Carter requests that you place completed correspondence and other work that you prepare for him on his desk in a manila folder. Correspondence prepared for his signature should be placed in this order, from top to bottom: original, any enclosures, and carbon copies. The envelope should be placed with the flap over the original, enclosures, and carbon copies so that the address on the envelope is visible. A paper clip is placed over the envelope. You should make an office copy of all materials that you prepare.

After the signed papers have been returned to you, you fold them and insert them into the appropriate envelopes. Interdepartmental memorandums are not placed in envelopes.

FILING

You are responsible for filing the office copy of typed material in the appropriate file. (As you prepare material in this project, you may place all office file copies in one file folder. Arrange them chronologically.)

1-D. THE OFFICE: A Decision-Making Center

One of the most exciting spots in a firm is in the office area because that is where decisions are made. To fulfill the obligations of her position, the executive secretary must be capable of intelligent execution of executive decisions, of assuming certain responsibilities, and of promoting good human relations within the firm and between her firm and other firms or persons.

In this exercise and in similar ones in other lessons, you will acquire a better understanding of the role of the executive secretary at the same time that you are improving your skill with the tools of communication.

After the signed papers have been returned to you by Doctor Mennen, you will be expected to fold them (if necessary) and insert them into the appropriate envelopes for mailing. You are responsible for filing the office file copy in the appropriate file. (As you prepare material in this project, you may place all office file copies in one file folder. Arrange the materials chronologically, with the most recent piece of correspondence on top.)

Doctor Mennen likes you to ask any *necessary* questions about a piece of correspondence immediately after he dictates it to you. Rather than bother him for the spelling of names or for correct addresses, you usually get such information from your files or from incoming correspondence. Since you will not have access to these sources in this project, you may verify the spelling of names and get addresses from the list in the following section.

ADDRESSES

These are the addresses that you will use for correspondence sent to individuals or firms who are located off the campus. They are listed alphabetically. You would normally get these addresses from incoming correspondence or from the office files.

Blackburn, Betty (Miss): 1110 Grandview Drive, Eugene, OR 97405

Blake, Janice (Mrs.): 438 Starlight Drive, NW, Salem, OR 97304

Kellermeyer, J K.: Professor, College of Business, Idaho State University, Pocatello, ID 83201

Langley, Calvin R.: President, Oregon State Business Education Association, 1515 Ames Way, SW, Portland, OR 97225

Leigh, Eleanor P. (Miss): Instructor, Department of Business Education, Billings Community College, Billings, MT 59101

Moore, Susan (Miss): Route 1, Box 161, Foster, OR 97345

Office Ink Products, Inc.: 1805 Fifth Avenue, SW, Portland, OR 97201

Parsons, Eugene A.: Publisher, *Business Careers*, 115 Madison Avenue, New York, NY 10022

Temple, Joanne (Mrs.): Instructor, Department of Business Education, Coos Bay Senior High School, Coos Bay, OR 97420

Wells, Patricia (Miss): Box 221, Gladstone, OR 97027

1-E. Executive Language

This type of exercise is intended to familiarize you with words or expressions commonly occurring in executive usage to facilitate your comprehending both oral and written communications. Study the explanations excerpted from a dictionary; learn the shorthand outlines; transcribe the notes.

qualitative (kwol' ə tā'tiv), adj. relating to quality or qualities.

qualitative analysis, a test designed to identify chemical components of a substance.

quantitative (kwon' tə tā' tiv), adj. 1. relating to quantity 2. that involving the measurement of quantity.

quantitative analysis, a test designed to determine the amount or proportion of a substance.

1-F. Internal Communications

These notes preview a memo that will be dictated.

maintenance, productive, technical, comprehend, frequently, pertinent, affixed, renewal, malfunction, persistent, effectiveness

PROJECT 1

BACKGROUND INFORMATION

In this project you will serve as secretary to Dr. H. T. Mennen, who is chairman of the Department of Office Administration at Western University in Salem, Oregon. The departmental office is located in 324 Troy Hall. Doctor Mennen has four colleagues in his department. They are:

Dr. Ruth Abbott, Professor (Office: 315 Troy Hall)
Dr. Mary L. Carson, Assistant Professor (Office: 317 Troy Hall)
Dr. James P. Pryor, Assistant Professor (Office: 321 Troy Hall)
Dr. Robert Wilson, Associate Professor (Office: 319 Troy Hall)

The Department of Office Administration is one of four departments in the College of Business. Dean Leonard S. Long is the administrative head of the College of Business. Dean Long's office is located in 100 Troy Hall.

In addition to handling administrative duties, Doctor Mennen also teaches courses in business education methods and business communication.

You are the only secretary in the departmental office suite. Your work station is located in the outer office. An inner office is occupied by Doctor Mennen. In the outer office you have an electric typewriter, a copying machine, a stencil maker, a stencil duplicator, and a spirit duplicator. (You have spirit masters onto which you can transfer a copy by running the original and a spirit master through the copying machine.)

SPECIAL INSTRUCTIONS

For his correspondence Doctor Mennen uses 8½" by 11" stationery. The letterhead contains the following information: Western University, Salem, OR 97301, Department of Office Administration, 324 Troy Hall, Telephone: (503) 335-3507. Doctor Mennen uses the block letter style and open punctuation. He does not use a subject line in his letters. He prefers *Sincerely* as a complimentary close and uses his name and title in the typed signature line. He prefers this style for reference initials: htm urs.

All on-campus correspondence is typed in memorandum form. Doctor Mennen uses the memorandum style that is illustrated on page i of the Appendix (Style 1). His memorandums are typed on plain bond paper. In on-campus memorandums it is customary to type only the name, the title, and the department in the To and From sections. Your employer expects you to provide an appropriate subject line for each memorandum.

All on-campus mail is placed in reusable 10" by 13" envelopes. Inserts are not folded. Off-campus mail is placed in No. 10 envelopes, which have a printed return address on them. These envelopes are put through a postage meter in the Central Mailing Department.

Doctor Mennen dictates most of his work to you soon after the morning mail delivery. He likes to have the completed correspondence and other work you prepare placed on his desk in a manila folder. He prefers to have correspondence prepared for his signature placed in this order: original, enclosures, and carbon copy or copies. The envelope is placed with the flap over the original, the enclosures, and the carbon copies so that the address side of the envelope is visible. A paper clip is placed over the envelope. You are expected to make an office copy of all material that you prepare.

LESSON 2

2-A. System Command

In the 20 standard words below there are 2 phrases and 10 Speedforms or derivatives.

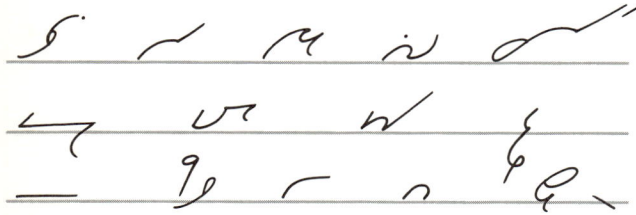

2-B. System Review

-ther, -thor
per-, pur-
sh
-sion, -tion
ou, ow
-ed
th

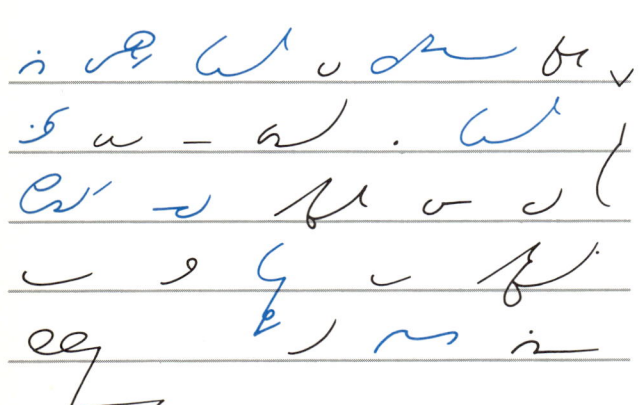

2-C. Recording Fidelity

2-D. THE OFFICE: A Decision-Making Center

70-D. Proofreading Exercise

The following letter contains 35 errors in grammar, spelling, punctuation, word division, word choice, letter style, consistency, or typewriting. Type a copy of the material as it appears below; then edit your typed copy, making the necessary corrections in pen or pencil. Begin the date on line 12 and leave a one-inch left margin.

November 31, 19--

Mr. Lawrence Perry
1 Villa Way
Minneapolis, MI 55436

Dear Mr. Perry:

Now you can see at a glance what you spend, and what you save with the First National Trust Bank's new Duo-Account.

With our new Duo-Account, Mr. Lawrence, you can have just one account number for both savings & checking. In this age of numbers, one fewer number certainly wont be missed!

With a new Duo-Account, your monthly statement of account will take on a new look. Your First National Trust Bank checking balance can still be scene at a glance with the same itemization-your begining balance, the number and total of the checks subtracted, the number and total of the deposits made, the amount of the resulting balance; and the amount of any service-charges.

In edition to the proceeding information, First National Trust Bank will also include a savings account summary on your monthly statement of account. This summary will include the amount of the beginning balance, the number and amount of withdrawals, the number and amount of deposits, the amount of the resulting balance, and the interest paid to date during the year.

Just say the word an you'll recieve a combined Duo-Account statement every month which will include your complete financial statas on one handy record.

If you are all ready a First National Trust Bank saver and you wish the new Duo-Account complete the enclosed form, and mail it to FNTB along with your pass book.

If you are not saving at FTNB at the present time, you may open a new account simply by using the form as your first savings' deposit slip. Your DuoAccount number will remain the same as your present savings account number. No new signature car is required to have both balances on one combined monthly statement.

Cordialy Yours,

J.P. Mc Clelland, President

JPM:vs

Efficient Arrangement of Desk Contents

LESSON 70

70-A. Special Problems

RECORDING AND TRANSCRIBING SPEECHES. A secretary may be asked to record from dictation a speech that her employer is preparing. Some individuals may be able to dictate a short speech in such a manner that it will require no revising or editing. In such a case, the secretary may transcribe her shorthand notes in final form immediately. For longer speeches the dictator probably will ask his secretary to prepare a draft of the speech. He may expect her to edit the speech for grammatical correctness as she prepares the draft. After all necessary revisions have been made, the secretary then types the speech in final form from the corrected draft.

70-B. Transcription Craftsmanship

TIPS ON TRANSCRIBING SPEECHES. The secretary should observe these pointers as she transcribes a speech:

1. Type the title in all capital letters. Single-space a title with more than one line and arrange it in inverted pyramid style. Triple-space after the title.

2. Use double spacing or triple spacing (according to the preference of your employer) for the body of the speech. Double spacing will make it easier for the speaker to follow his notes as he delivers the speech.

3. Use a large type style for the final copy of the speech if your employer prefers it to your conventional type style.

4. Allow an extra half inch for the left margin if the speech is to be bound at the side; otherwise leave margins of equal width.

5. Number the first page of the speech in the middle at the bottom of the page. Number the succeeding pages in the upper right corner.

70-C. Transcription Problem

Speech
(to be dictated)

Background: You are the secretary to a vice-president of the First National Bank. Your employer has been asked to speak to a basic business class in a local high school. He dictated the speech to you, and you prepared a typewritten draft for him. He has made many changes on the draft. Since his revisions are hard to read, he decides to dictate the speech to you again from the revised draft.

Instructions: Transcribe the speech that your instructor will dictate to you. Please follow the instructions that are given in 70-B and observe these preferences of your employer: He would like to have this speech double-spaced. He would like to have you use conventional type for your transcript. He does not wish to have the speech bound. He wants an original and one carbon copy of the speech. He will dictate the title to you. You need not edit the speech, since he has already done so.

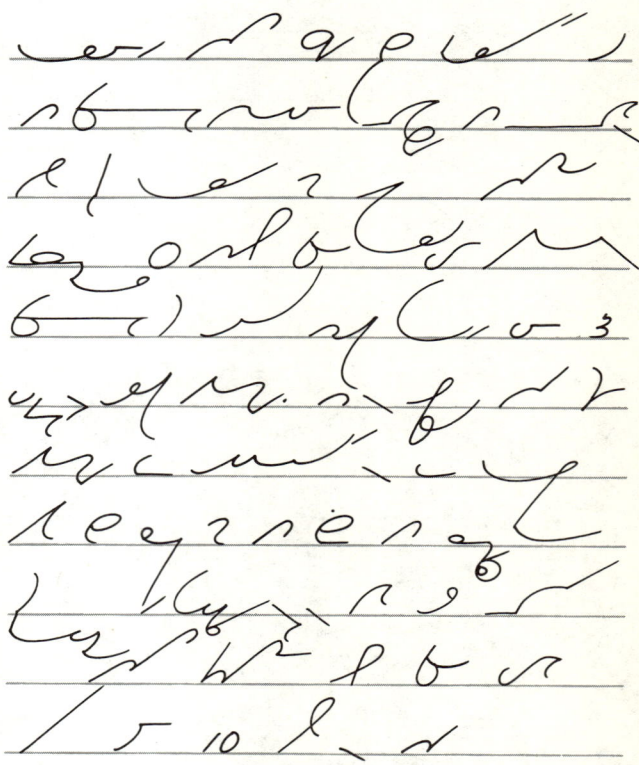

Letter 2
(Office-Style Dictation)

Dictator: Wayne S. Lidner, Accountant

Addressee: Mr. R. E. Krause, Manager, Lee Business Forms, P. O. Box 160, Mason City, IA 50401

Background: Mr. Lidner is reporting errors on invoices sent by Lee Business Forms, which resulted in overcharges to First National Bank.

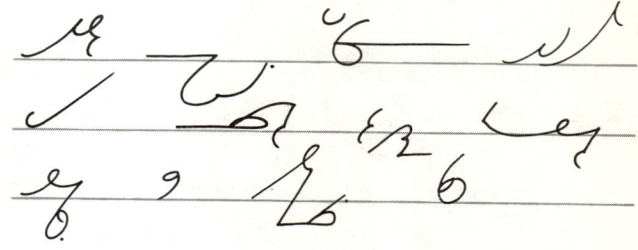

invoices, imprinting, overpayment, vouchers, audit, mathematics, substitution, clerks, verifying, issue, designating, payee

Lesson 69

2-E. Executive Language

innovation (in′ ə vā′ shən), n. 1. change made in established way of doing things 2. new idea or device.

potentiality (pə ten′ shē al′ ə tē), n. 1. potential state or quality; possibility as opposed to actuality. 3. ability to develop or come into existence.

productivity (prō′ duk tiv′ ə tē), n. 1. power to produce 2. the quality of being productive.

2-F. Internal Communication

critical, subprofessional, serviceable, inevitably, drastic, reduction, semester, supervisor, academic, emergency, unprecedented, financial, devised, librarian's

LESSON 3

3-A. System Command

In the 20 standard words below there are 5 phrases and 13 Speedforms or derivatives.

3-B. System Review

-er, -or
dd, dt, td

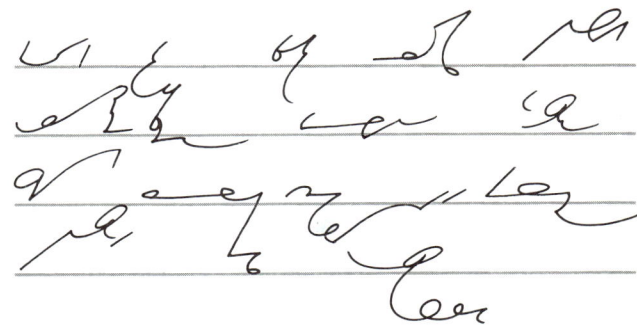
-tual, -tuel
mm, mn, -ment

69-C. Executive Language in Banking

collateral (kə lat′ ər əl), adj. guaranteed by property, stocks, or bonds.

foreclose (fôr klōz′), v. to deprive a mortgagor the right to redeem mortgaged property.

corroborate (kə rob′ ə rāt), v. to confirm.

69-D. Communication in Banking

Use the modified block letter style with mixed punctuation for the letters in this lesson.

Letter 1

Dictator: K. A. Potter, Vice President

Addressee: Mr. Lawrence P. Jones, 2401 Beech Court, Detroit, MI 48239

Background: Mr. Potter is informing Mr. Jones that foreclosure proceedings will be instituted on his mortgage unless delinquent payments are made soon.

3-C. Recording Fidelity

3-D. THE OFFICE: A Decision-Making Center

Mail Rough Sorted

Lesson 69

Letter Ready for Dictator

Mail Being Opened

Mail on Dictator's Desk

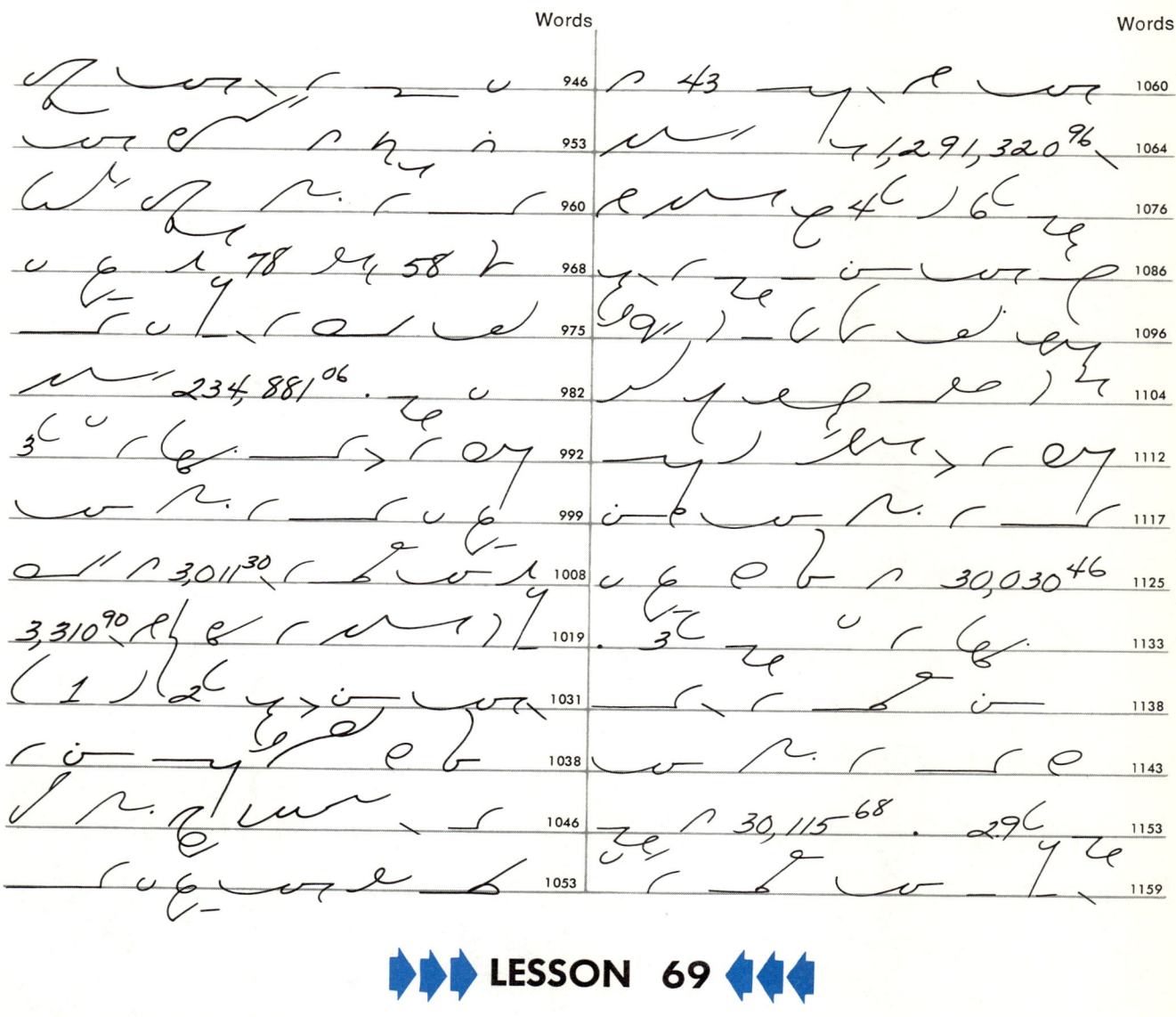

LESSON 69

69-A. System Control

This exercise, dealing with banking services, contains 150 standard words. Your instructor will dictate it to you several times until you can record it fluently.

69-B. THE OFFICE: A Decision-Making Center

3-E. Executive Language

ecology (ē kol' ə jē), n. a branch of science concerned with the relation of organisms to their environment and to each other.

priority (prī or' ə tē), n. 1. quality of coming before. 2. precedence according to order of importance. 3. legal precedence in exercise of rights.

purport (pər pôrt), v. 1. convey outwardly. 2. to intend; profess.

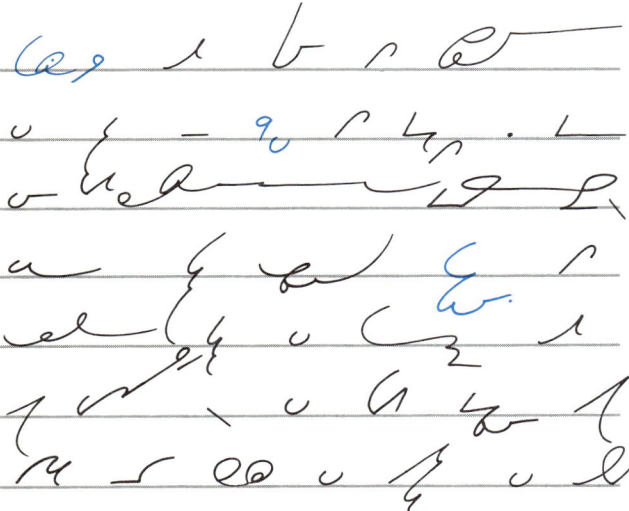

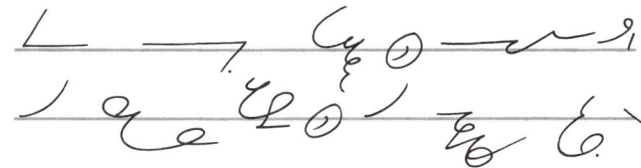

3-F. Internal Communication

steadily, conformity, regulations, estimated, necessitated, excluding, preferably, reuse, obliterated, discernible, preruled, bundles, University, identity, identifiable, Addressograph, mailings, multiple-station

LESSON 4

4-A. System Command

In the 20 standard words there are 4 phrases and 13 Speedforms or derivatives.

4-B. System Review

al-
dm, dn
-graph

Lesson 68 — Page 217

-gram

nd, nt, nv

tm, tn

tran-, trans-

4-D. THE OFFICE: A Decision-Making Center

4-C. Recording Fidelity

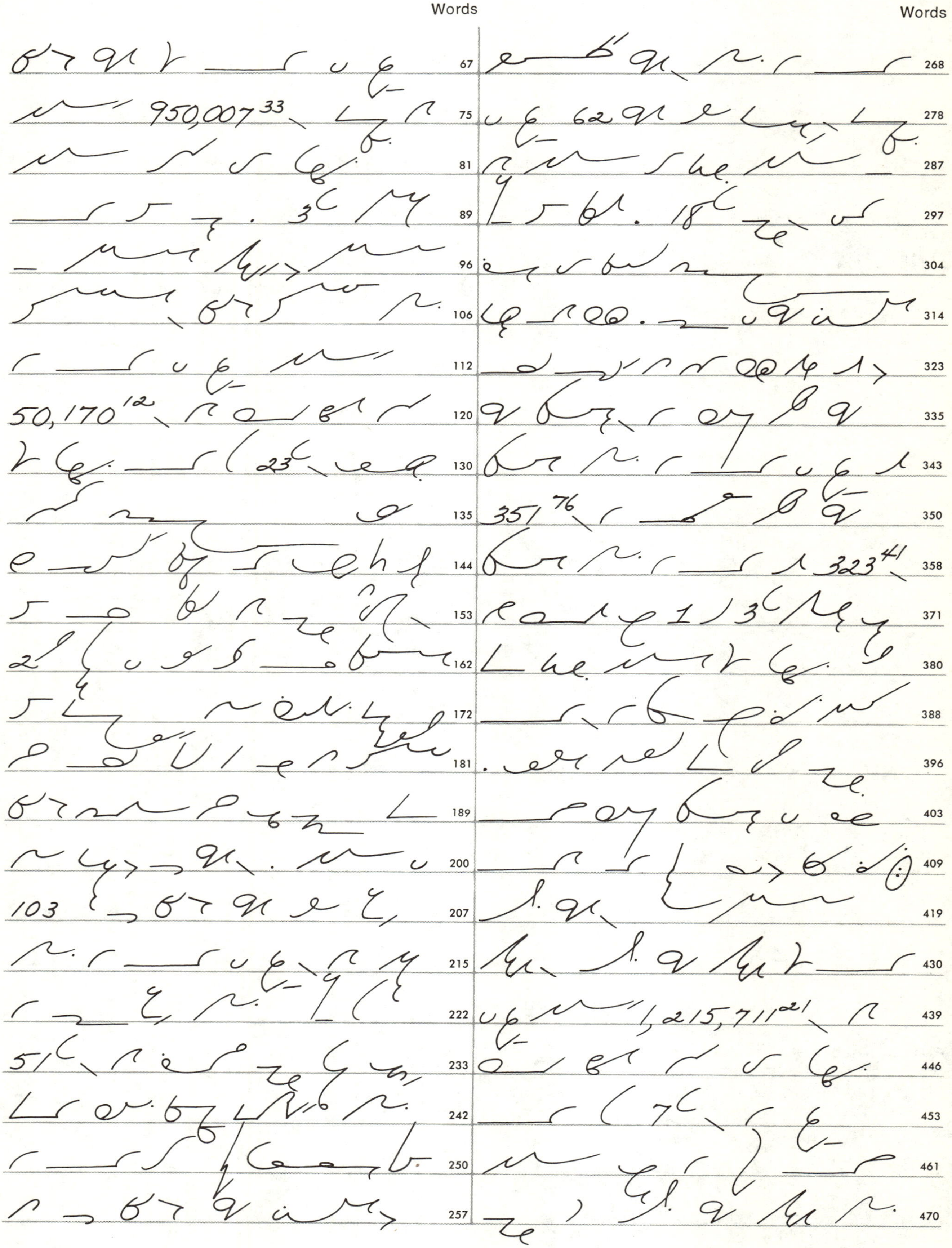
Words
Words
67
75
81
89
96
106
112
120
130
135
144
153
162
172
181
189
200
207
215
222
233
242
250
257
268
278
287
297
304
314
323
335
343
350
358
371
380
388
396
403
409
419
430
439
446
453
461
470

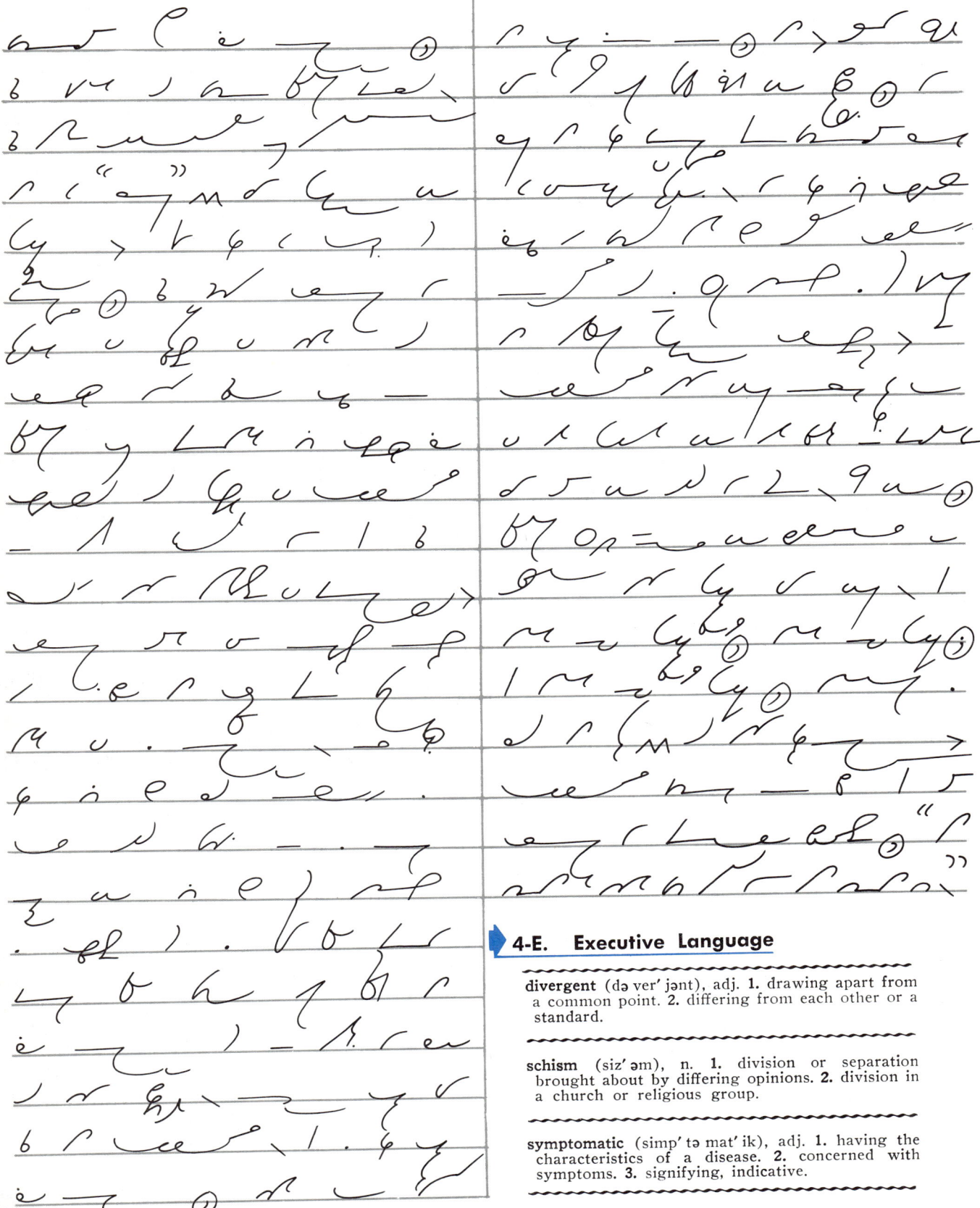

4-E. Executive Language

divergent (də ver' jənt), adj. **1.** drawing apart from a common point. **2.** differing from each other or a standard.

schism (siz' əm), n. **1.** division or separation brought about by differing opinions. **2.** division in a church or religious group.

symptomatic (simp' tə mat' ik), adj. **1.** having the characteristics of a disease. **2.** concerned with symptoms. **3.** signifying, indicative.

Letter 2
(Office-Style Dictation)

Dictator: A. P. Montgomery, Trust Officer

Addressee: Mrs. K. S. Lane, 233 Banyan Drive, Jackson, MS 39211

Background: Mr. Montgomery is informing Mrs. Lane that she has inherited some personal effects and a sum of money from a distant relative.

LESSON 68

68-A. Special Problems

THE MEMORANDUM REPORT. Many short business reports are typed in memorandum style. A major style difference between the memorandum report and the conventional memorandum is the use of centered, side, and paragraph headings. These headings orient the reader to the topics to be presented in the various sections. Such headings also help the reader to locate specific data quickly, without having to scan the entire report.

68-B. Transcription Craftsmanship

TIPS FOR TYPING MEMORANDUM REPORTS. An acceptable memorandum report style appears on page i in the Appendix. Notice the arrangement of the section headings. To avoid confusion, one should be consistent as he composes and types the headings. The headings should be parallel in structure. A sufficient number of appropriate headings should be used so that unrelated data do not fall under an inappropriate caption.

A triple space should precede and follow major centered headings. A triple space should precede and a double space should follow side headings. A double space should precede paragraph headings.

68-C. Transcription Problem

Memorandum Report

Background: C. P. Carr, a vice-president of the First National Bank, has the responsibility of preparing a monthly report on the Bank's savings account, checking account, and loan activity. He has dictated to you the following memorandum report for the month of September. You are to transcribe the report in the format that is presented on page i of the Appendix. Prepare one carbon copy.

4-F. Internal Communication

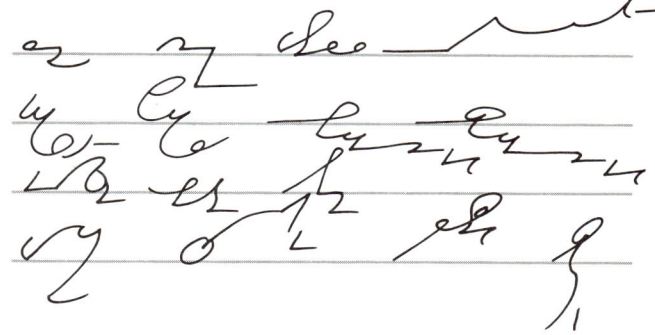

ensure, uniform, stationery, Midlands, Cooperative, appropriate, macrocommunications, microcommunications, continuation, requisition, definition, stenographer, identification, deviations, typographical

LESSON 5

5-A. System Command

There are 10 phrases and 22 Speedforms or derivatives in the 40 standard words below.

5-B. System Review

ex-
nk

com-
ya

-ive, -sive, -tive
in-

67-C. Executive Language in Banking

escrow (es' krō), n. a deed, bond, or some written agreement deposited with a third party until some condition is fulfilled by two other parties.

amortize (am' ər tīz), v. to set money aside regularly to pay a debt when it is due.

equity (ek' wə tē), n. the value remaining beyond any liability or mortgage.

67-D. Communication in Banking

Use the modified block letter style with mixed punctuation for the letters in this lesson.

Letter 1

Dictator: A. P. Montgomery, Trust Officer

Addressee: Mr. Jack L. Winston, Attorney, 1429 Peachtree, N.W., Atlanta, GA 30309

Background: Mr. Montgomery is writing to Mr. Winston to secure information about a deed that the attorney is holding in escrow.

5-C. Recording Fidelity

5-D. THE OFFICE: A Decision-Making Center

Lesson 67

Page 213

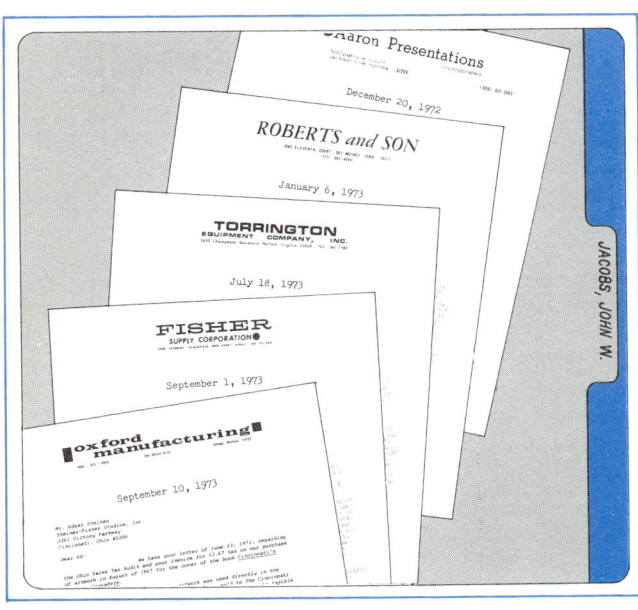

Proper Order of Filed Papers in a File Folder

Removing a Folder from the Files

LESSON 67

67-A. System Control

67-B. THE OFFICE: A Decision-Making Center

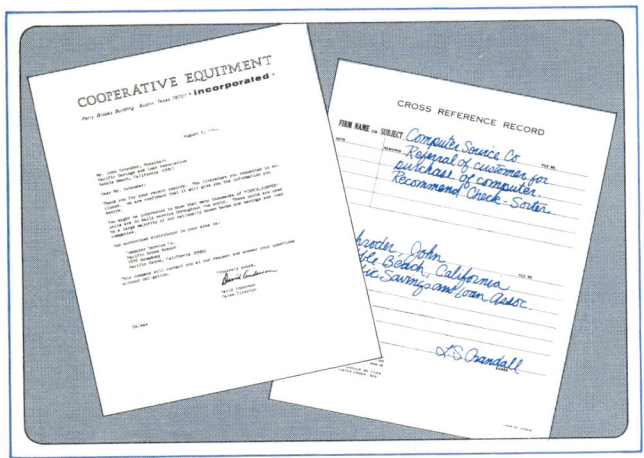

Letter and Its Cross Reference

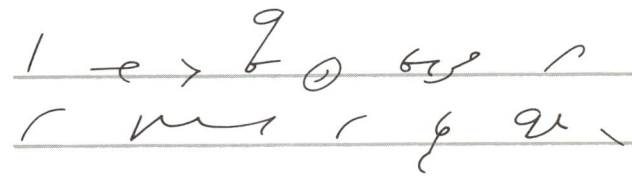

5-E. Executive Language

perfunctory (pər fungk′ tə rē), adj. 1. performed in a routine manner; mechanical. 2. lacking in enthusiasm; apathetic.

simulation (sim′ yə lā′ shən), n. 1. process of feigning. 2. imitation; counterfeit.

supportive (sə pôrt iv), adj. furnishing support.

5-F. Internal Communication

maximum, conveniently, periodicals, pamphlets, relevant, housed, Extension, Oxford, translations, scientific, departmental

Lesson 5 Page 18

66-B. Proofreading Exercise

The following letter contains 35 errors in grammar, spelling, punctuation, word division, word choice, letter style, consistency, or typewriting. Type the material as it appears in this exercise; then edit your typed copy, making the necessary corrections in pen or pencil. Begin the date on line 12 and leave a one-inch left margin.

April 18, 19--

Prof. Ruth Cramer
Department of Business Education
College of Oregon
Salem, OR 97303

Dear Professor Cramer

Your "A Day In The Office" program for Business Education seniors sounds like a worth while experience for perspective office employees. We would be happy to have three of your students as "guest employees" in the Old National Bank on May 12. We will make an effert to see that these girls will have an opportunity to get an over view of the operations in our executive offices, and to see the roll of the secretary in a bank office. We will also see that they have an opportunity to utilize the knowlege and skills they have learned in school in an on the job situation.

Please send us the name of the students who plan to visit us by May 7; and we will then have identification tags already for them, when they arrive.

Mrs. Shirley Nelson, whose my executive secretary, will meet the girls at 8:45 a.m., on Wednesday morning, in our office, room 511. After a breif orientation, she will take them to the secretaries who they will be working for during the day.

We expect that your students will wonder about appropriate dress for the occassion. Because of the nature of our business, our secretaries tend to dress conservative.

Our office hours extend from 9 a.m. untill 5 p.m. Most of our employees eat thier lunch in our cafateria. We would like to have the girls be special guests of the bank at lunch. The secretaries will act as hostess for the luncheon.

Should anybody drive, they can park in the Bank's employee parking lot.

If the students have any questions please have them call Mrs. Nelson.

Sincerely yours

John S. Warren
Vice President - Personel

jsw sn

LESSON 6

6-A. System Command

There are 10 phrases and 26 Speedforms or derivatives in the 40 standard words below.

6-B. System Review

-ing

con-

-cation

-acle, -ical, -icle

-ology

y   ye-

cents 50¢ hundred 3 5 dollars 1 5 1

-bility

6-C. Recording Fidelity

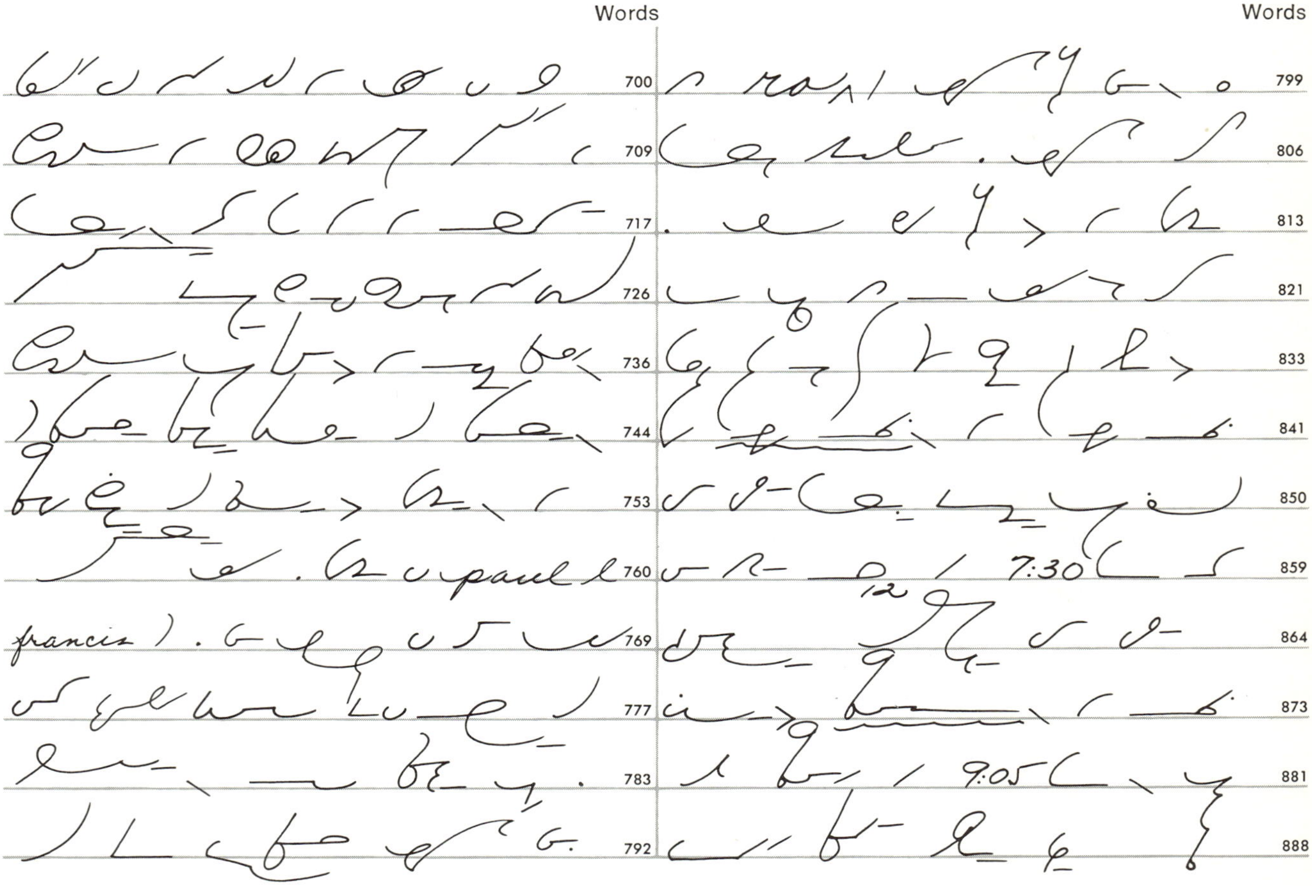

LESSON 66

66-A. Transcription Problems

Background: You are to assume that you are a stenographer in the office of John J. Jackson, president of the First National Bank, located in the First National Bank Building in Lincoln, Nebraska. An advisory board has been established, comprised of six prominent citizens from across the state. Your job involves the preparation of an agenda and minutes for the initial meeting of the group.

Problem 1—*Agenda* (to be dictated)

Pauline Carson, executive secretary for Mr. Jackson, dictates an agenda for the first meeting of the Advisory Board on September 4, 19--, at 1 p.m. in the Board of Directors Room. She asks you to prepare a draft in triplicate. Copies of this draft will be submitted to the president and the chairman of the board for approval. Use the agenda format presented in Lesson 65 and prepare an appropriate heading.

Problem 2—*Minutes* (to be dictated)

Miss Carson recorded the minutes for the first meeting of the Advisory Board. She now dictates them to you and asks you to type them in good form. Prepare the minutes in triplicate so copies may be sent to Mr. Flake and Mr. Jackson for their approval before their final distribution. Use the format in Lesson 65 and prepare an appropriate heading. Type the closing lines, including a blank line for Mr. Flake's signature. (Mr. Flake is chairman of the Advisory Board.) Indicate the action taken on any motions under their respective marginal headings.

UNIT 13 COMMUNICATION IN BANKING

6-D. THE OFFICE: A Decision-Making Center

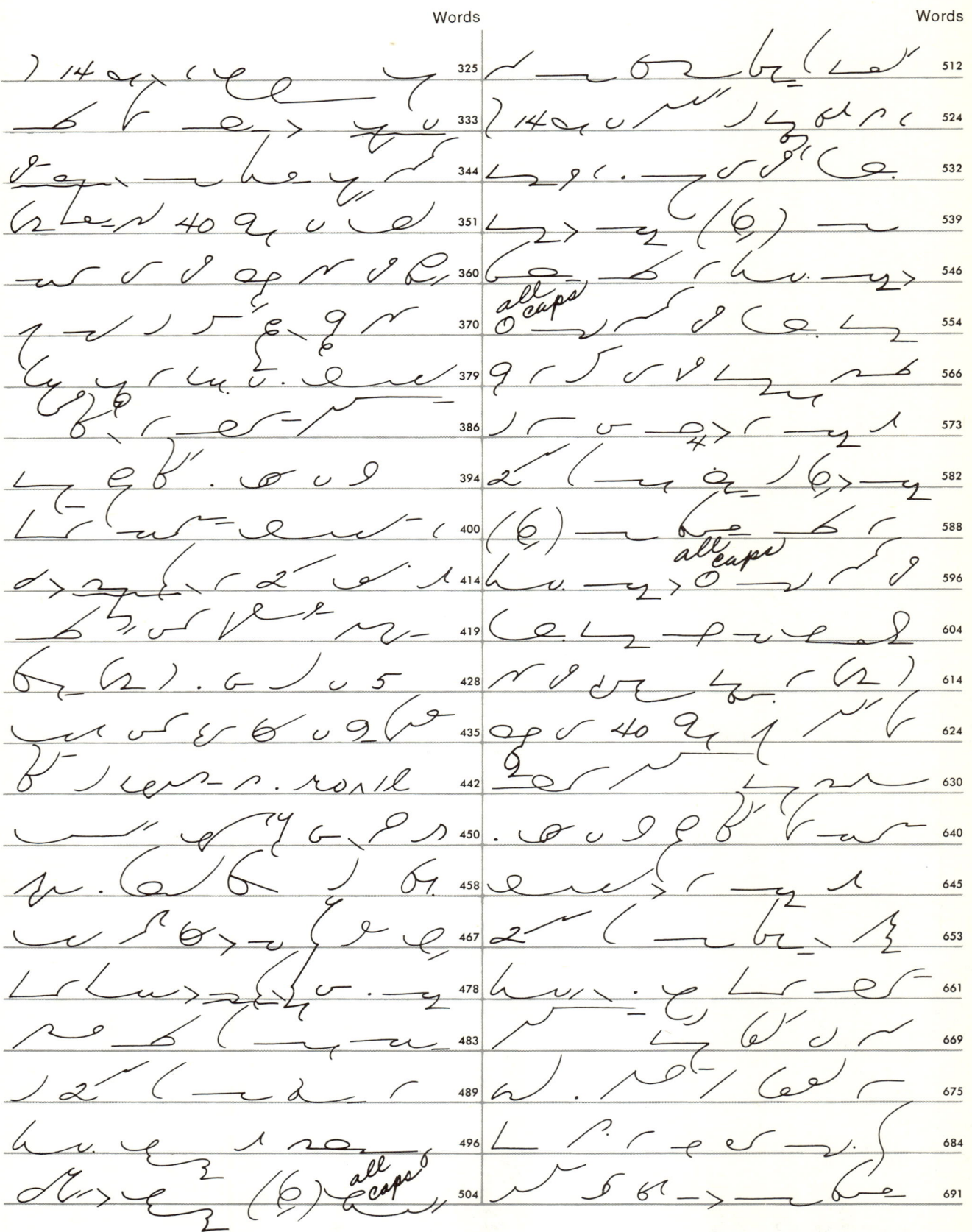

6-E. Executive Language

feedback (fēd' bak'), n, **1.** the return of a portion of the output to the input of a system or process. **2.** information about the result of a process.

ineffectual (in' ə fek' chủ əl), adj. **1.** not producing the correct or desired effect or response. **2.** a futile attempt.

obsolescent (ob' sə les' nt), adj. **1.** becoming obsolete; out of date; unable to compete with more recent models. **2.** going out of use.

Lesson 6 — Page 21

Minutes

Transcribe the following minutes, which you recorded for the April 11 meeting of the City Planning Commission. Use the format illustrated on the preceding page. Include a space for your signature, your employer's signature, and date on which your employer approved the minutes.

6-F. External Communication

These shorthand notes preview two extra-office letters that will be dictated. Practice writing the outlines to increase your rate of taking dictation.

expensive, continually, achievements, pharmaceutical, indication, desperately, virus, infections, malaria, worldwide, observations, specialist, handicapped, rehabilitation, bimonthly, horizons, forthcoming, invaluable

LESSON 7

7-A. System Command

There are 7 phrases and 19 Speedforms or derivatives in the 40 standard words below.

-ologist

i followed by a basic vowel

7-B. System Review

ld

un-

-ject

gr, jr

ng

-ship

style appears below. Note the following points:

1. Marginal headings are used to enable one to locate information quickly.

2. A secretary records the time and place of the meeting and the roll call even though such business is not formally stated in the meeting.

3. Verbatim motions and amendments are typed in capital letters to give them prominence.

4. One of the following notations is placed under the marginal heading for a motion to indicate the action that has been taken on it: (passed), (defeated), (not seconded), or (tabled).

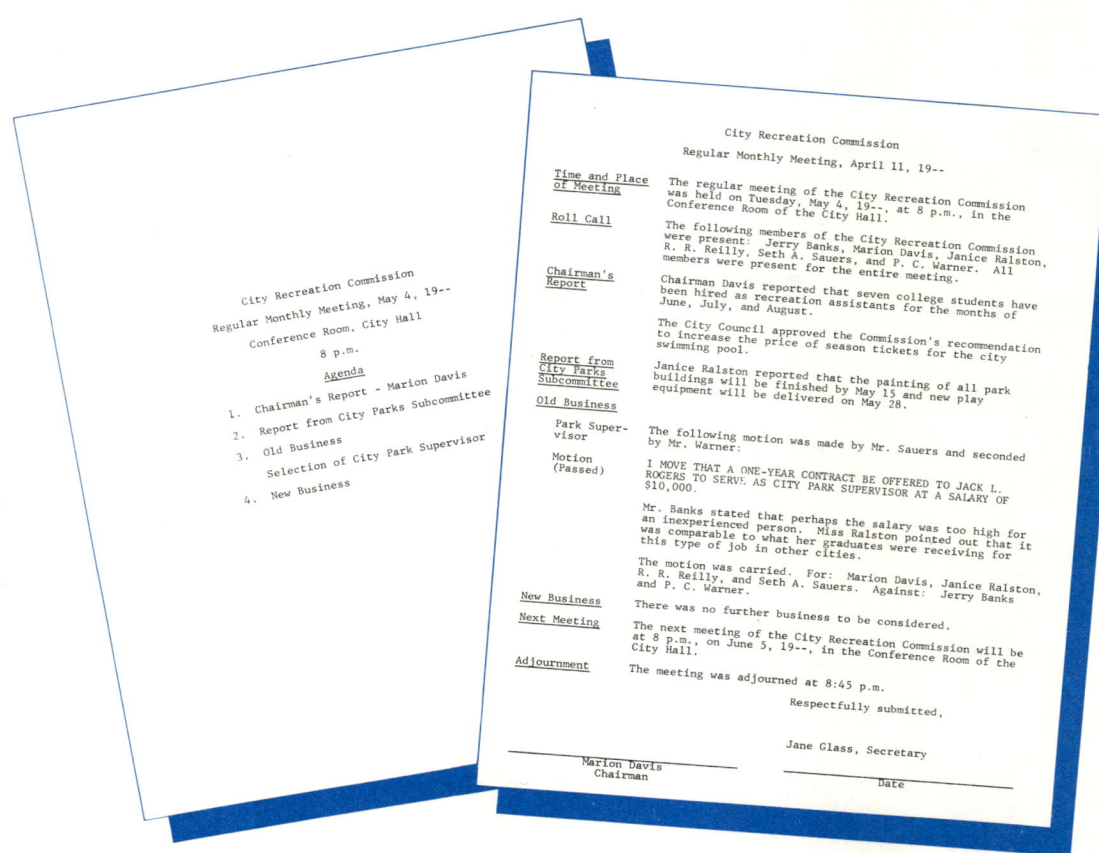

Agenda and Minutes

65-C. Transcription Items

Agenda

You are secretary to the chairman of the City Planning Commission. Transcribe the following agenda, which your employer has dictated to you. Use the format illustrated above.

Lesson 65 Page 207

7-C. Recording Fidelity

7-D. THE OFFICE: A Decision-Making Center

Letter 2
(Office-Style Dictation)

Dictator: Q. R. Trent, Chairman

Addressee: Mr. and Mrs. J. S. Reynolds, Box 441, Drummond, MT 59832

Background: Mr. Trent, chairman of the Clear Lake Improvement Association, is notifying some Drummond citizens about an impending meeting of the group.

LESSON 65

65-A. Special Problems

AGENDA. When a secretary notifies individuals about an impending meeting, she often includes an agenda with the notice. The agenda indicates the reports that will be called for and the topics that are scheduled for discussion at the meeting.

MINUTES. As a secretary, you may be called upon to record minutes of meetings and transcribe them in acceptable form for official records. You may also be asked to record and transcribe minutes dictated to you by another individual who attended a meeting at which you were not present.

If you are asked to record the minutes of a meeting, you may wish to follow these practices:

1. Study the agenda ahead of time. Have all files and records that might be needed with you.

2. Have minutes of previous meetings available for reference purposes.

3. Record the names of all individuals present for the meeting, if required.

4. Sit where you can observe and hear all the participants in the meeting.

5. Record all significant points in the proceedings.

6. Ask to have points about which you are not clear restated.

7. Record verbatim all motions, amendments, and resolutions. Restate them for verification, if possible.

8. Record the names of individuals who make motions and those who second motions.

9. Record the votes of participants, if required.

10. Collect written reports for use in preparing your minutes. (Written reports are sometimes attached to the minutes.)

11. Record the times at which late-comers enter the meeting and the times at which individuals leave the meeting prior to adjournment, if required.

65-B. Transcription Craftsmanship

TIPS ON TYPING AN AGENDA. The chairman of the meeting will probably prepare a draft of an agenda, which you then will type in final form. An acceptable format for an agenda appears on the following page.

TIPS ON TRANSCRIBING MINUTES. Various styles are used to prepare minutes. A secretary should determine whether a prescribed style has been authorized. A commonly used

Lesson 65

64-C. Executive Language in Public Administration

primary election (prī′ mer′ ē i lek′ shən), n. a preliminary election.

general election (jen′ ər əl i lek′ shən), n. an election held to make a final selection for office from candidates elected in a preliminary election.

incumbent (in kum′ bənt), n. one who holds an office.

64-D. Communication in Public Administration

Use the block style and open punctuation for the letters in this lesson.

Letter 1

Dictator: Kenneth L. Klein, City Clerk

Addressee: T. K. Grossman, 1131 Appaloosa Drive, Boise, ID 83705

Background: The City Clerk is answering a request for information from a prospective candidate for the City Council.

7-E. Executive Language

compatibility (kəm pat′ ə bil′ ə tē), n. 1. quality of being compatible. 2. capable of existing in harmony; agreement.

interim (in′ tər im), n. an intervening time; a pause. adj. temporary.

optimal (op′ tə ml), adj. most desirable; favorable.

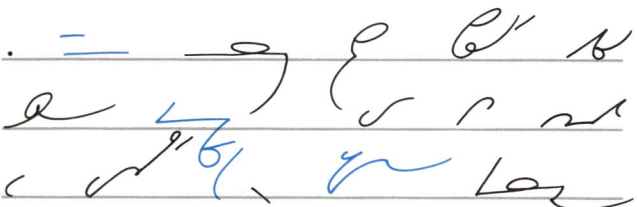

7-F. External Communication

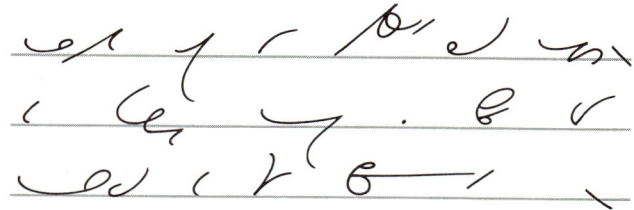

surrounding, community, Concert, dedicated, adult, choral, classics, contemporary, pianist, youthful, baritone, newcomers

▶▶▶ LESSON 8 ◀◀◀

8-A. System Command

There are 9 phrases and 13 Speedforms or derivatives in the 20 standard words below.

8-B. System Review

oi, oy

electric, electr-

-ings

over

o'clock 9ᵘ 11ᵘ 3ᵘ

-titude, -titute

under

sub-

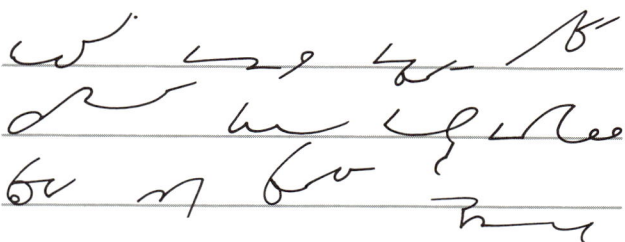

Lesson 8 — Page 25

8-C. Recording Fidelity

8-D. THE OFFICE: A Decision-Making Center

LESSON 64

64-A. System Control

The material in this dictation exercise deals with a refuse disposal plan proposed for Central Idaho. There are 150 standard words in the article. Your instructor will dictate it until you can record it fluently in one minute.

64-B. THE OFFICE: A Decision-Making Center

[shorthand content]

63-D. Proofreading Exercise

The following letter contains 35 errors in grammar, spelling, punctuation, word division, word choice, letter style, consistency, or typewriting. Type a copy of the material as it appears below; then edit your typed copy, making the necessary corrections in pen or pencil. Begin the date on line 12 and leave a one-inch left margin.

June 31, 19--

Kirk C. Rogers
1212 S. Spring Street
Pittsburg, KA 66762

Dear Mr. Rogers

Your letter of June 14 to Mr. Carson City Superviser has been refered to me. I realize that the dust problem on your new street makes an unpleasant situation. Let me assure you that you're problem is not unique. On nearly all of the unpaved streets in new sections of the city we have situations where nonresidents of a particular area also use the street therby increasing the dust problem even more for the residence concerned. I think the best way to answer your letter is to tell you first what we cannot do, and then what we can do.

Although this question comes up every year about this time, the city is not able financialy to oil unpaved streets with in the city limits. Where local residents wish to oil the gravel streets theirselves, we do make an effort to cooperate by scrapeing the street just prior to the oiling operation. We also hold of as long as possible before we rescrape the oiled surface.

The Pittsburgh City Council is concerned with getting existing unpaved streets up to paved standards, but although our new sub-division standards provide for temporary paving by the sub-divider, it will take a while to catch up on those streets that presently do not have an oiled surface.

I shall ask our Superintendent of Public Works to look at the portion of Rogers Street, on which you live, to see if there is an adequate cover of crushed rock on it. In the event that rock need to be added we shall do this as soon as it can be schedulled.

                                                           Sincerely yours

                                                           R.K. Barbour,
                                                           City Engineer

cc: Superintendant of Public Works

RKB/tsu

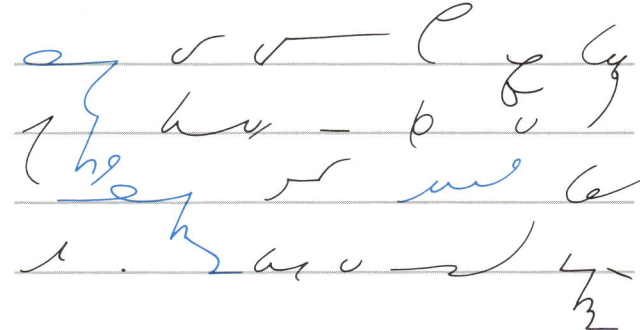

8-F. External Communication

8-E. Executive Language

ambiguity (am' bə gū ə tē), n. 1. quality of being ambiguous. 2. capable of having more than one meaning. 3. uncertainty; doubt.

malfunction (mal funk' shən), vi. 1. to function imperfectly. 2. to fail to operate in the usual manner. n. act of malfunctioning.

warranty (wôr' ən tē), n. 1. something which authorizes or justifies; warrant. 2. a promise or guarantee of the integrity of a product; manufacturer's responsibility for repairs or replacements.

publicly, balloons, augmented, carnival, competitive, unusual, fascinating, effective, accompanying, documents, administrative, Cincinnati, reminder, invoices

LESSON 9

9-A. System Command

There are 10 phrases and 26 Speedforms or derivatives in the 40 standard words below.

9-B. System Review

-ful
im-
inter-, intr-
-ological
-ulate
-ward
self

Letter 2
(to be dictated)

Dictator: (same as Letter 1)

Addressee: R. L. Roscoe, Attorney at Law, 1702 Douglas Street, Omaha, NE 68102

Background: Mr. Taylor is requesting legal counsel from Mr. Roscoe about dismissing a city employee.

maintenance, disappointment, hesitate, encouraging, language, neglected, transistors, integrity, supervisor, threatens, unfair, dismissing

Letter 3
(to be dictated)

Dictator: (same as Letter 1)

Addressee: Dennis Spencer, City Street Supervisor, City Building Annex, Omaha, NE 68102

Background: Mr. Taylor is asking Mr. Spencer to check into complaints some citizens have made about chuckholes in a city street.

property, chuckholes, Footwear, angle, Victory, beyond, occasions, protective, thereafter, obligated, assure, improvements

Lesson 63

9-C. Recording Fidelity

9-D. THE OFFICE: A Decision-Making Center

LESSON 63

63-A. Special Problems

CUTTING CORRESPONDENCE COSTS. It is estimated that the cost of a typical personally dictated business letter is approximately three dollars. To reduce the cost of such correspondence, businessmen sometimes use one or more of the following practices: (1) substitute a telephone call for a letter, (2) type the answer to a routine inquiry at the bottom of the incoming letter, (3) use form letters when they are appropriate, (4) have their secretaries compose letters when possible, and (5) use carbon set forms that provide space for both a message and a reply. The latter forms come with one-time carbon inserts or as no-carbon-required sets.

63-B. Transcription Craftsmanship

TIPS ON TYPING MESSAGE AND REPLY FORMS. A message and reply carbon set usually contains three sheets—an original and two copies. The originator of a message and reply form types his comments in the message section of the form. He then detaches the last copy of the set for his files and sends the original copy, along with the first copy, intact to the addressee. The addressee types his answer in the reply section of the form. He then returns the original copy and detaches the remaining copy, which bears both the message and the reply, for his files. An illustration of a message and reply form is shown on page iv in the Appendix.

63-C. Transcription Letters

Prepare your own typed message and reply carbon sets, using the illustration on page iv in the Appendix. Use the block letter style and open punctuation for the letters in this lesson. Prepare appropriate subject lines.

Letter 1

Dictator: L. J. Taylor, City Manager, City Building, Omaha, NE 68102

Addressee: Joseph Law, City Park Supervisor, City Building Annex, Omaha, NE 68102

Background: Mr. Taylor is asking Mr. Law to take some action to prevent the pilferage of bricks in one of the city parks.

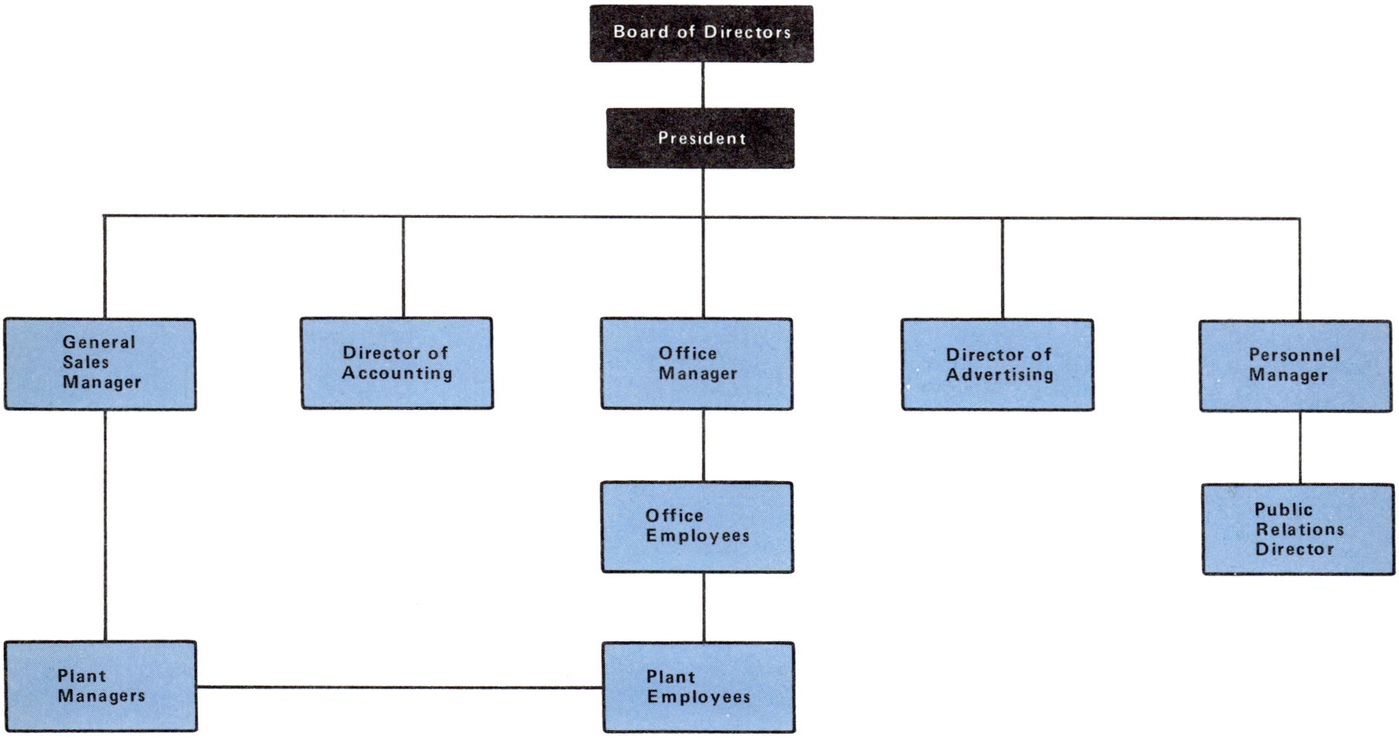

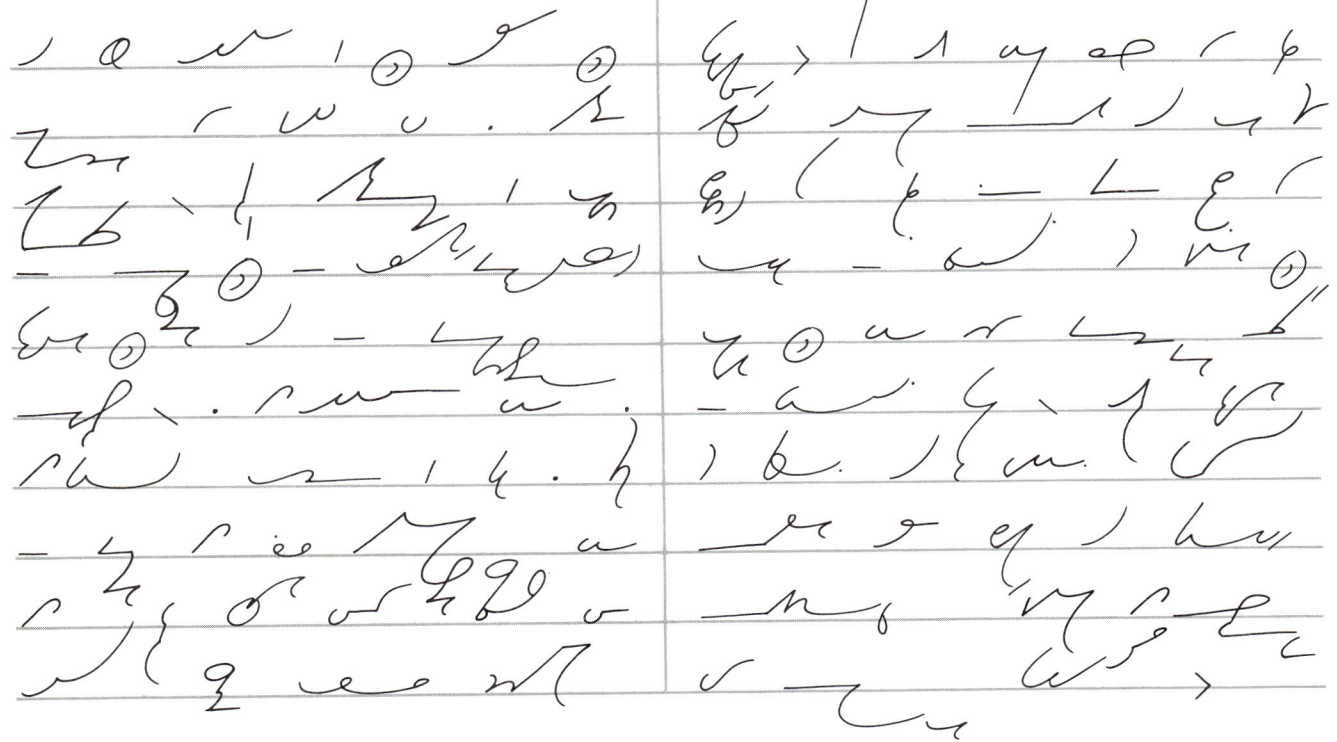

Organization Chart

Lesson 9

Page 30

county agent about the field trips the commissioners will be making.

Letter 2
(Office-Style Dictation)

Dictator: C. E. Gordon, Chairman

Addressee: Mayor Donald D. Pelton, City Building, Denver, CO 80202

Background: The state Joint Municipal Committee chairman is notifying Mayor Pelton of a hearing to be held in his city.

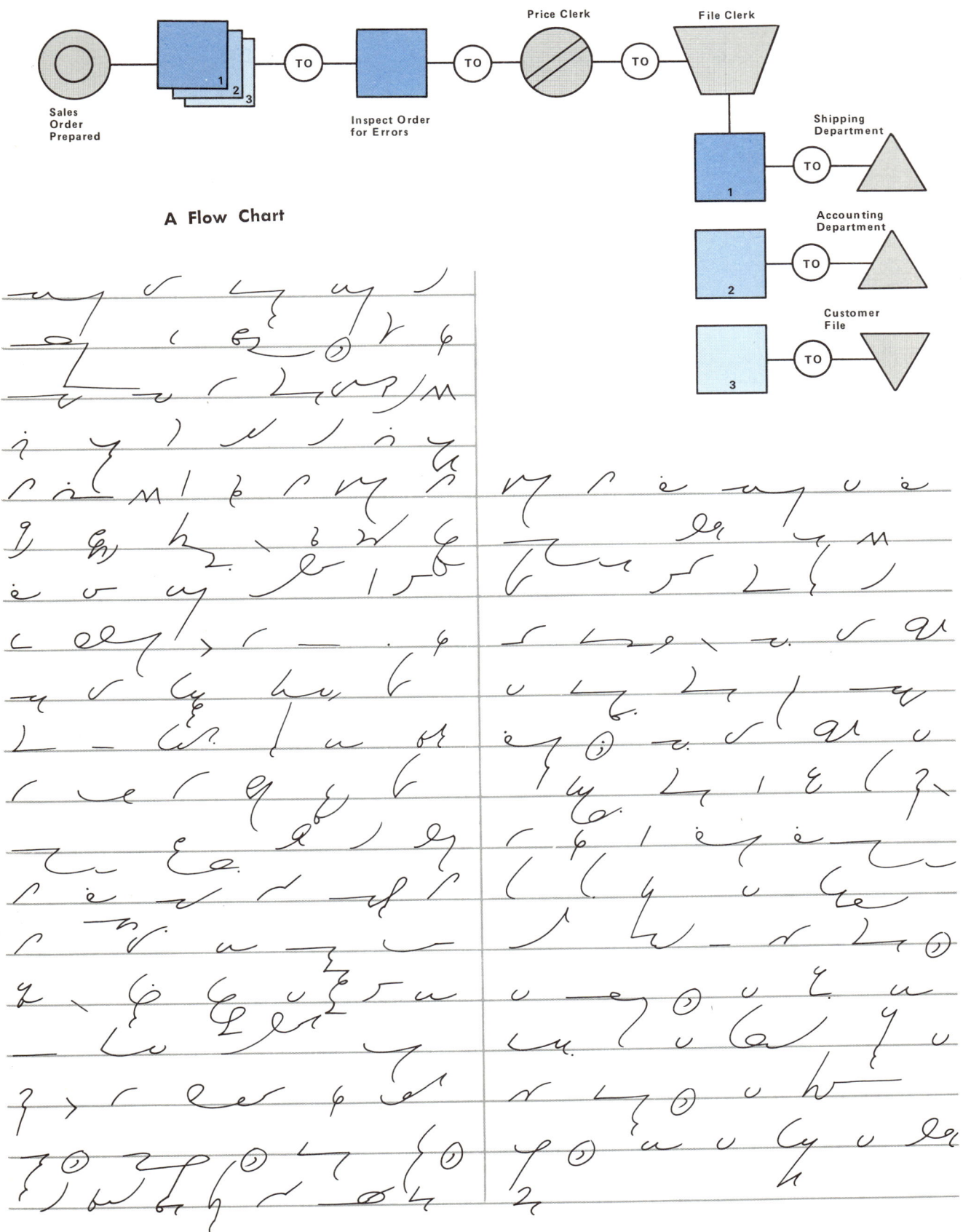

A Flow Chart

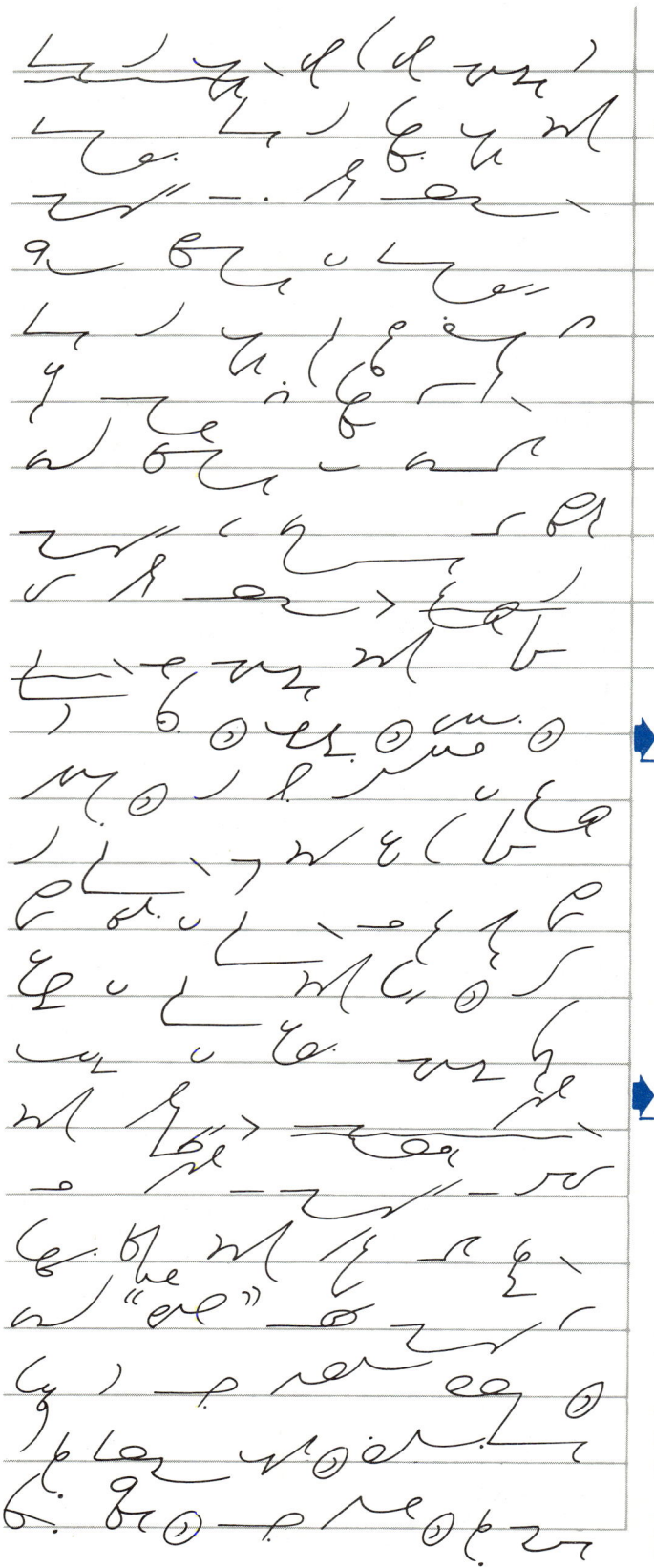

62-C. Executive Language in Public Administration

ordinance (ôrd′ nəns), n. a law of a municipal or county body.

holdings (hōl′ dings), n. property held by legal right.

sanctuary (sangk′ chú er′ ē), n. place of refuge or protection.

62-D. Communication in Public Administration

Use the block letter style and open punctuation for the letters in this lesson.

Letter 1

Dictator: T. S. Lockwood, Chairman

Addressee: Clarence S. Sims, County Extension Agent, Fuser County Courthouse, Saint Joseph, MO 64501

Background: The Chairman of the Board of County Commissioners is informing the

9-E. Executive Language

component (kəm pō′ nənt), adj. serving or helping to compose or constitute. n. an essential part or ingredient.

corroborate (kə rob′ ə rāt), v. 1. to confirm or support with evidence. 2. to make more certain.

incompatible (in′ kəm pat′ ə bl), adj. 1. unable to act together in harmony. 2. unsuitable for use together; opposed in character or components.

9-F. External Communication

binder, presentation, jewelry, junk, electroplating, realistic, structures, brochure, stuffers, particulars, bracketed, miscellaneous, excluding, crossword, puzzles.

Lesson 10

10-A. System Command

There are 6 phrases and 13 Speedforms or derivatives in the 20 standard words below.

10-B. System Review

-ous, -us

-hood

million /50 /4 billion /3

super- supr-

-script

-sation, -zation

10-C. Recording Fidelity

10-D. THE OFFICE: A Decision-Making Center

LESSON 62

62-A. System Control

Your instructor will dictate to you a short article about city budgeting procedures. It contains 150 standard words. Practice taking this dictation until you can record it fluently in one minute.

62-B. THE OFFICE: A Decision-Making Center

[shorthand]

61-D. Proofreading Exercise

The following letter contains 35 errors in grammar, spelling, punctuation, word division, word choice, letter style, consistency, or typewriting. Type a copy of the material as it appears in this exercise; then edit your typed copy, making the necessary corrections in pen or pencil. Begin typing on line 12 and leave a one-inch left margin.

Mayor Eldon Tyson
Municipal Building
City

Dear Mayor Tyson

Here are the results of the preliminary survey that you requested the City Civil Service Comission to make to determine how municipal employees feel about the present policy, that allows bonus points to be added to promotional testscores when the examinee has achieved additional education credits.

Our staff distributed three hundred questionnaires to a stratified sample of city employees which included 20 per cent of the citys' supervisors, 20 per cent of the municipal labors and office workers, and 20 per cent to the public safety employees. A total of 168 questionnaires was returned.

Of the employees' returning questionaires, 57 percent favored the retention of the rule that allows education credit bonus points on promotional civic service examinations. Approximately 14 per cent favored changing the policy. 28 per cent of the respondants wished to see the rule elimenated.

The figures that denote disatisfaction with the present system should not be interpreted to mean that city employees are strongly opposed to education credits. The majority of the city employees, expecially the uniformed services, emphaticly supports education. The main objection to the rule is the manner in which education achievment is recognized and awarded. The unformed services desire a remunerative type recognition while the non-uniformed services have not taken a strong position as to what method they desire.

The City Civil Service Commision continue to take the position that additional education achievment by city employees should be recognized and entered on there personel records. Such information should then be taken into consideration when evaluating an employee's work performance or when considering an employee for promotion.

                Cordially Yours

                Civil Service Examiner

Approved_____
    Cheif, Civil Service Commission

ATS:lm

10-E. Executive Language

acquisition (ak′ wə zish′ ən), n. 1. act of acquiring. 2. object which has been acquired or gained.

determinant (di tėr′ mə nənt), n. a factor, cause or situation which determines or conditions the outcome of something.

mobility (mō bil′ ə tē), n. 1. state of being mobile, capacity for movement. 2. adaptability to new surroundings.

10-F. External Communication

chartered, tax-exempt, experimentation, noteworthy, philanthropic, fellowships, endowment, launch, deductible, distinguished, superb, exemplifies, logical, empirical, donations, solicitations, scholarship

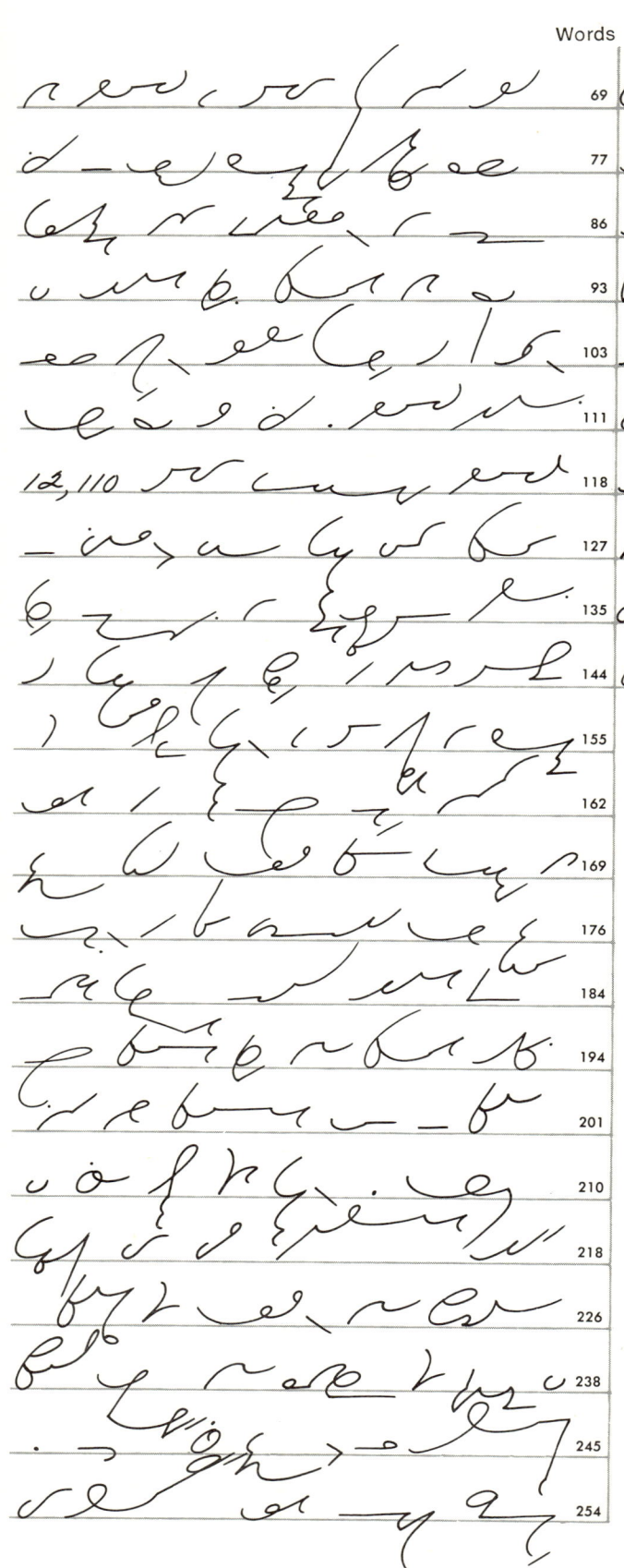

Letter 2
(to be dictated)

Dictator: Mrs. Alice Rogers, Office Manager, City Treasury Office

Addressee: Mr. James Casper, 1201 Libby Road, Norwalk, CT 06850

Background: Mrs. Rogers is notifying Mr. Casper of the termination of his appointment. The letter must be approved by the Mayor of Norwalk.

Letter 3
(to be dictated)

Dictator: Miss Jeanne Pettit, Licensing Clerk

Addressee: Lt. Peter Purcell, 1411 Sheldon Avenue, Colorado Springs, CO 80904

Background: Miss Pettit is answering an inquiry from Lt. Purcell concerning a new all-terrain vehicle license. The letter must be approved by the chief of the Licensing Bureau.

LESSON 11

11-A. System Control

Facility in phrasing promotes speed in note-taking. A *family* of *he will* phrases appears in the notes below. After becoming familiar with the shorthand by reading the material and practicing the phrases, try to build a high dictation speed.

11-B. THE OFFICE: A Decision-Making Center

"The statis of employes with senority of 20 years has been undergoing study, and our decisions are as follows ..,"

"Pittsburg,"

LESSON 61

61-A. Special Problems

APPROVAL LINES. In some firms and governmental offices an approval line is included in certain types of correspondence. This line bears the signature of an individual other than the person who signs the letter. The approval line may be required for one or more of the following reasons: (1) It may serve as written evidence that the action taken in the letter has been officially authorized. (2) It may serve as a precautionary measure to ensure that confidential material is not sent to unauthorized individuals. (3) It may also serve as a safeguard to ensure the reader that the information contained in the letter is correct.

61-B. Transcription Craftsmanship

TIPS ON TYPING APPROVAL LINES. Type the approval line at the left margin a double space below the reference initials. Type the appropriate title below the signature line. An acceptable style is illustrated below:

```
                              Sincerely,


                              Robert P. Poland, Office Manager

RPP:lts

Approved  _____
                Executive Vice-President

Enclosure
```

61-C. Transcription Letters

Use the block letter style and open punctuation for the letters in this lesson. Each letter will require an approval line.

Letter 1

Dictator: E. P. Harris, Clerk of Elections

Addressee: Mayor John Powell, City Building, Knoxville, MD 21758

Background: In this letter Mr. Harris is reporting the official returns in the recent city election. The letter is to be approved by the chairman of the Board of Elections.

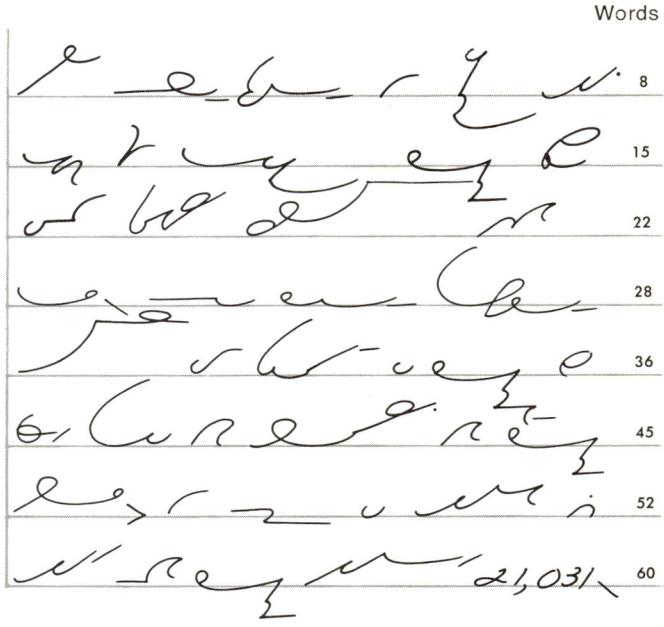

UNIT 12 COMMUNICATION IN PUBLIC ADMINISTRATION

Note space to indicate two separate words

Accent mark (also indicates end of a syllable)

Hyphen mark   **Syllable break**

con sole¹ (kən sōl′), v.t., -soled, -sol ing. ease the grief or sorrow of; comfort: *I tried to console the lost child.* See **comfort** for synonym study. [< Middle French *consoler* < Latin *consolari* < *com-* + *solari* soothe] —**con sol′a ble**, adj. —**con sol′er**, n.
con sole² (kon′sōl), n. 1 part of an organ containing the manuals, stops, and pedals. 2 panel of buttons, switches, dials, etc., used to control electrical or electronic equipment in a computer, missile, etc. 3 a radio, television, or phonograph cabinet, made to stand on the floor. [< French. beam, support]

us visible < *conspicere* specere look] —**con**
—**con spic′u ous ness**,
con spir a cy (kən spir
1 act of conspiring; secre
ers to do something un
pecially against a gove
sonage, etc. 2 a plot or
con spir a tor (kən sp
who conspires; plotter.
con spir a to ri al (kə
spir′ə tōr′ē əl), adj. ha
spiracy or conspirators.

railroad/train.
state's evidence, 1 evidence brought forward by the government in a criminal case. 2 U.S. testimony given in court by an accused person against his alleged associates in a crime. 3 **turn state's evidence**, U.S. testify in court against one's alleged associates in a crime.
States-Gen er al (stāts′jen′ər əl), n. the legislative body of France from 1302 to 1789, consisting of representatives of the three estates, the clergy, the nobility, and the middle class; Estates-General.
state side (stāt′sīd′), INFORMAL. —adj.

sta tion (stā′shən), n.
son is appointed to occ
ance of some duty; assi
took his station at the
2 locality or post assigne
a person or unit. 3 place
assigned and where equ
some particular kind of
the like: *a postal stati*
4 the police headquarte
regular stopping place:
road station. 6 depot.
New Zealand) a cattle or
or equipment for send

sta tion ar y (stā′shə ner′ē), adj. 1 having a fixed station or place; not movable. 2 standing still; not moving. 3 not changing in size, number, activity, etc.
station break, pause in a radio or television program, or between programs, to identify the broadcasting station or network.
sta tion er (stā′shə nər), n. person who sells paper, pens, pencils, ink, etc. [< Medieval Latin *stationarius* shopkeeper, originally, stationary, as distinct from a roving peddler]
sta tion er y (stā′shə ner′ē), n. writing materials such as paper, cards, and envelopes.
station house, police station.

2 state; condition: *Diplo*
the status of world affa
to stand. Doublet of ST
status quo (kwō′), t
existing state of affairs.
which]
stat ute (stach′üt), n.
legislative body. See **lav**
2 a formally established
establish < *stare* to star
statute mile, mile (de
statute of limitatior
the time during which ri

Lesson 11

News Release 2
(to be dictated)

Dictator: John T. Robinson, General Manager KWLT and KWLT-TV, P. O. Box 1116, Raleigh, NC 27602 (Telephone: 567-3305)

Addressee: The Raleigh News, P. O. Box 2019, Raleigh, NC 27602

Background: Mr. Robinson is announcing to the press the merger of KWIK and KWLT-TV stations. This information is for immediate release.

listeners, transition, appreciative, modernization, renovated, electrification, conduit, fixtures, hedge

News Release 3
(to be dictated)

Dictator: Leonard P. Stone, Editor, The Daily Times, P. O. 1711, Seattle, WA 98111 (Telephone: 542-6619)

Addressee: KWSI-TV, P. O. Box 2200, Seattle, WA 98111

Background: Mr. Stone is announcing the appointment of a new manager for the Personnel Department of The Daily Times. This information is for immediate release.

Seattle, doctorate, dissertation, chemistry, counselor, discharged, infantry, Korea, trustees

non-, *prefix.* not; not a; opposite of; lack of; failure of: *Nonessential* = not essential. *Nonresident* = not a resident. *Nonconformity* = lack of conformity. [< Latin < *non* not] If an adjective formed with *non-* is not defined in this dictionary, its meaning will be clear if *not* is put in place of the *non*. If a noun formed with *non-* is not defined, its meaning will be clear if *not*, *not a*, *the opposite of*, or *the absence of* is put in place of the *non*. *Non-* is a living prefix and may be used with any noun, adjective, or adverb; but if there is a commonly used word of the same meaning formed with *un-*, *in-*, or *dis-*, that word is usually preferable. Most of the words that have *non-* as the preferred usage, or as a respectable rival of *un-*, are listed below, or as regular entries.	non/ab sorb/ent non ac/a dem/ic non/ad dic/tive non/ad her/ence non/ad he/sive non/ad ja/cent non/ad min/is tra/tive non/ad mis/sion non/ag gres/sive non/a gree/ment non ag/ri cul/tur al non/ap pear/ance non/a quat/ic non/as sess/a ble non/as sim/i la/tion non/ath let/ic non/at tend/ance non/au thor/i ta/tive non ba/sic non be/ing

11-C. Professional Language in Education

The following words appear in the dictation in 11-D. Usage of these words is not limited to education, but they occur frequently in communications in that field.

kickoff (kik' ôf'), *n*. **1.** a beginning; commencement. **2.** kick that puts a ball into play.

provisional (prə vizh' ən l), *adj*. provided for temporary need; conditional.

retreat (ri trēt'), *v*. to withdraw. *n*. **1.** act of withdrawing from something dangerous. **2.** signal for retreat. **3.** a private place or refuge.

11-D. Communication in Education

BACKGROUND FOR COMMUNICATION #1. The Board of Student Organizations has an annual banquet to which it invites students who have been elected to serve as presidents of the various student organizations on campus the coming year. In its letter of invitation, the Board wants to emphasize the services it provides so that each newly elected leader will want to attend the function.

of each page after the first page. Center the word *more* at the bottom of each page except the last page.

6. To indicate the end of the article, center three number signs with alternate spaces in this manner: # # #

60-C. News Releases

Use the style illustrated on page vi in the Appendix for the news releases in this lesson. Type them on standard-size paper. Leave 1½-inch side margins. Compose appropriate titles for the news releases.

News Release 1

Dictator: E. M. Harris, Programming Director, KWII-TV, P. O. Box 236, Billings, MT 59103 (Telephone: 332-1720)

Addressee: The Billings Gazette, P. O. Box 2311, Billings, MT 59103

Background: Mr. Harris is sending publicity on a television series to the local newspaper.

BACKGROUND FOR COMMUNICATION #2. An organization under provisional status is to be informed that its operations are to be reviewed for possible permanent status. Study the preview before taking dictation.

provisional, status, evaluation, Social, Calendar, Regulations, submission, financial, sponsors

BACKGROUND FOR COMMUNICATION #3. Miss Holder cannot attend the Presidents' Banquet. She wants the Board of Student Organizations to know she has a legitimate excuse for declining. The letter is dictated in "office style."

LESSON 12

12-A. Effective Display Guidelines

PAPER—THE "CARRIER" OF COMMUNICATIONS. The paper on which a message is written "carries" that message to the addressee. It plays a vital part in creating a favorable first impression. As we all know, sandwiches served on a beautiful tray look more delicious than ones served on a sheet of cardboard. Recognizing the value of that good first impression, the firm selects carefully the paper on which its communications are to be transmitted.

Papers available for both external and internal communication differ in size, weight, quality, finish, color, and grain.

The most commonly used size of paper for letters and memos is 8½ by 11 inches, although many other sizes are used; and many firms use more than one size. Some other commonly used sizes are 7¼ by 10½, 8½ by 7¼, 8 by 10½, and 8½ by 5½.

The most frequently used weights of paper for communications are 16-, 20-, and 24-pound, with 20-pound being the most commonly used.

"Twenty-pound" paper means that a manufacturer's ream of 500 17- by 22-inch sheets weighs 20 pounds. This paper cut in any size is referred to as 20-pound paper, and a package of it would be labeled "Substance 20" or "Sub. 20."

All paper has a right and a wrong side. The right side of the paper is called "felt"; the wrong side is called "wire." A good quality

Letter 2
(to be dictated)

Dictator: John L. Carey, Editor

Addressee: Mrs. W. P. Grace, 1512 Oak Street, Fall River, MA 02720

Background: Mr. Carey is answering a complaint about excessive advertising in his magazine, <u>Household</u>.

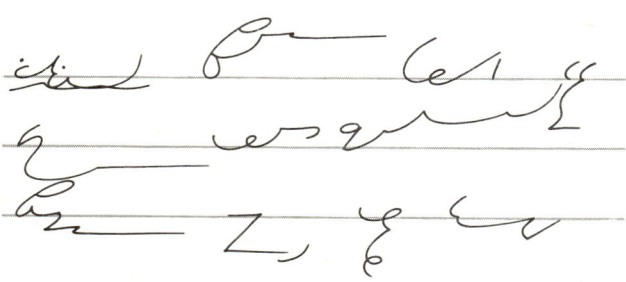

<u>Household</u>, abandonment, periodical, subscription, supplement, revenue, equivalent, apportionment, informative, recipes, solicit

Letter 3
(Office-Style Dictation)

Dictator: K. V. Miles, Manager

Addressee: Mr. T. S. Thomas, 1917 Lee Avenue, Reading, PA 19607

Background: Mr. Miles, a theater manager, is explaining the film rating system to a patron.

Divinity, theater, apologize, audience, revolution, inappropriate, unobjectionable, self-censorship, prominently, previews

LESSON 60

60-A. Special Problems

NEWS RELEASES. Occasionally your employer may wish to submit a news item to the press. You will then prepare a news release. If many news releases are issued by your firm, special news release forms may be available. If not, you will type the release on standard-size bond paper. A release date is always typed on a news release so that the editor will know the earliest date on which the item can be published.

60-B. Transcription Craftsmanship

TIPS ON PREPARING NEWS RELEASES. A model news release appears on page vi in the Appendix. These points should be kept in mind as you prepare a news release:

1. On a line 1½ inches from the top of the sheet, type the name, address, and telephone number of your firm and also the name and title of the individual who may be contacted if further information is needed.

2. At the left margin a double space below the preceding information, type the release date. Use whichever information is appropriate: FOR IMMEDIATE RELEASE or FOR RELEASE ON (date).

3. Triple-space below the release date and center an appropriate title in all caps.

4. Triple-space below the title and begin typing the article. Use double spacing and leave wide margins so that the editor will have space to make notations.

5. If the article requires more than one page, center the page number at the top

of paper has a watermark on it that you can see by holding the sheet of paper toward the light. The side on which you can read the watermark is the right side for typing.

Paper made entirely from wood pulp is called "sulphite"; paper made from cotton fibers is called "rag." The better the quality of the paper the greater the rag content. Paper selected for extraoffice communications is usually at least 25% rag content. Stationery which is used in top-echelon offices may be 50% or more cotton content. Legal and other documents that must be kept indefinitely are usually typed on paper that is 100% rag.

Various finishes of paper are available such as smooth, ripple, or cockle. Most paper used in business offices has a smooth finish.

Usually stationery for extraoffice letters is white, although some specialty firms (such as a flower shop) may use a tinted paper. With the advent of the optical scanner in some metropolitan post offices, the U.S. Postal Service is urging firms to use white or very lightly tinted paper since the scanner "reads" an address better with maximum contrast between the paper and the typed words.

The grain of paper may be "short" or "long." "Short" means the grain goes across the width of the paper; "long," the length of the paper. Short-grain paper is usually selected for individually typed messages; it bends to the curve of the typewriter platen. The long-grain is preferred for duplicating paper; it has less tendency to "roll over" as it is fed through the duplicator.

12-B. Transcription Craftsmanship

EFFICIENT NOTE READING. One aspect of swift, accurate transcription is the efficient reading of shorthand notes. By reading in "thought phrases," you will not need to reread your notes; and you will not misread the notes because you will be getting the thought as you transcribe.

In the sentences below, the colored perpendicular lines mark the notes into thought phrases. Insert two sheets of typing paper into your machine. Set the margins for a 60-space line with single spacing. Read the first phrase; then type it, keeping your eyes on the notes. Type each succeeding phrase in the same way.

the Committee on Committees of the Faculty Senate its recommendations for changes in its own membership.

DIRECTIONS TO THE TRANSCRIBER. Use 8½ by 11 bond paper. Since the bulletin will be duplicated, no carbon copy is necessary. Type each of the three numbered recommendations in the bulletin as a separate paragraph. Read in thought phrases as you transcribe. Center the heading, BULLETIN #1, on the 15th line from the top of the page. Double space to the subheading and center it; type the subheading in initial caps. Triple-space to the body of the message. Use a 60-space line and single spacing within paragraphs. Use a 5-space paragraph indention.

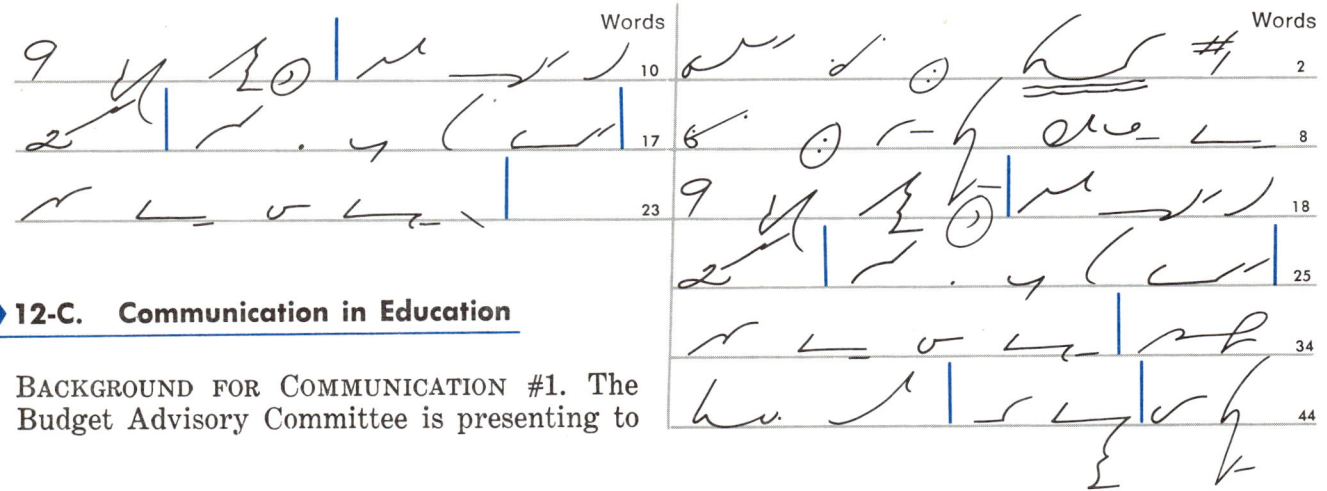

12-C. Communication in Education

BACKGROUND FOR COMMUNICATION #1. The Budget Advisory Committee is presenting to

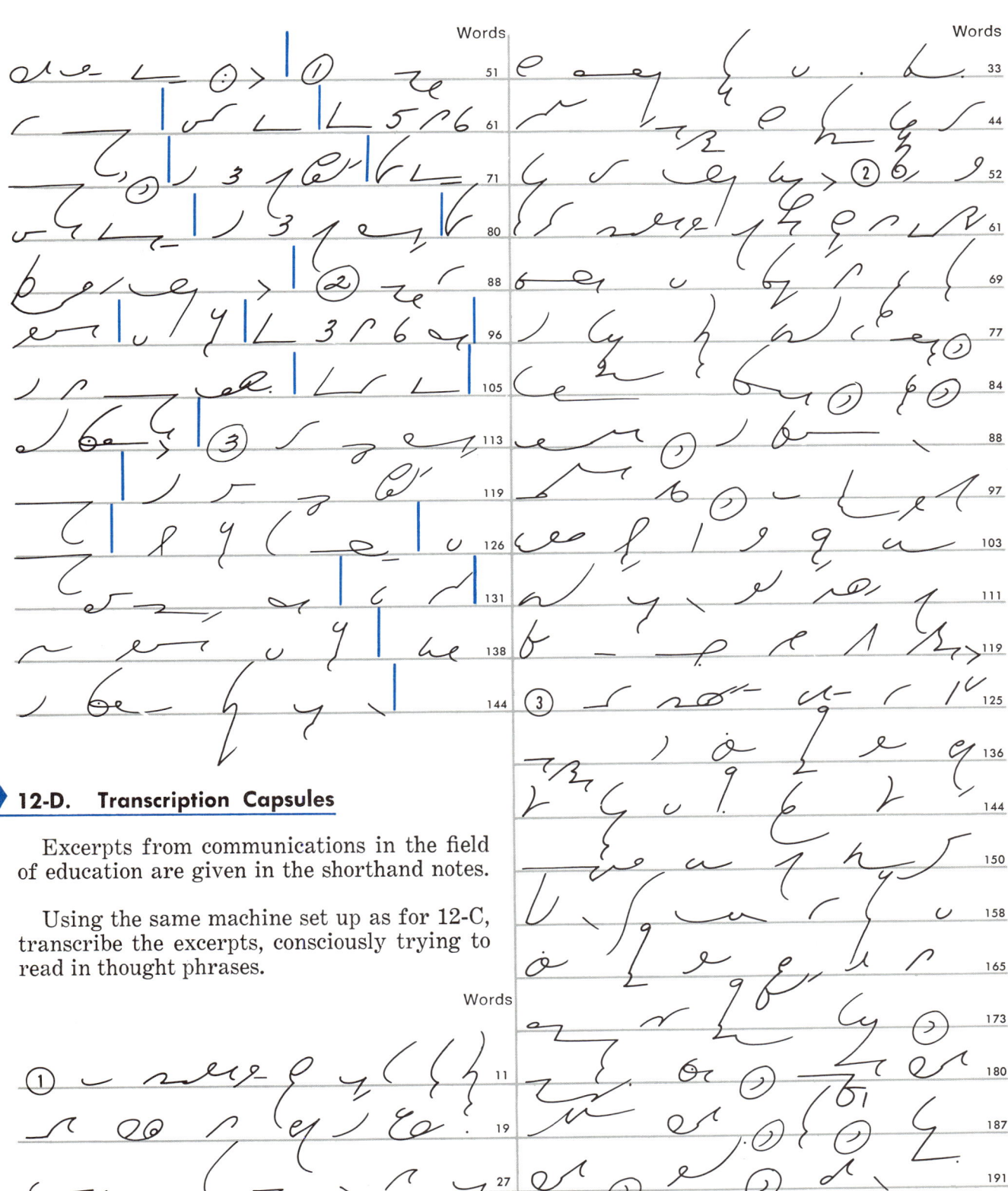

12-D. Transcription Capsules

Excerpts from communications in the field of education are given in the shorthand notes.

Using the same machine set up as for 12-C, transcribe the excerpts, consciously trying to read in thought phrases.

59-C. Executive Language in Mass Media

boom (büm), n. a long movable arm used to transport a microphone in a radio or television station.

cut-in (kut' in), n. a short network news report interpolated in a local broadcast.

transcription (tran skrip' shən), n. a recorded radio or television broadcast.

59-D. Communication in Mass Media

Use the modified block style and mixed punctuation for the letters in this lesson.

Letter 1

Dictator: P. L. Kent, Station Manager

Addressee: Miss Cynthia Brandon, 1411 Gayle Street, Portland, OR 97222

Background: Mr. Kent is answering a request about careers in the television industry.

LESSON 13

13-A. System Control

The notes provide for automatization of seven phrases beginning with the word *about*.

13-B. THE OFFICE: A Decision-Making Center

Lesson 59

13-C. Professional Language in Education

> **cardinal** (kärd' n əl), adj. of main importance. n. 1. high official of the Roman Catholic Church. 2. a bright red. 3. cardinal bird. 4. cardinal number.
>
> **sabbatical leave,** one-year leave granted to professors for rest, research, or travel.
>
> **tenure** (ten' yər), n. 1. the act, right, or manner of possessing, as land, or position.

13-D. Communication in Education

BACKGROUND FOR COMMUNICATION #1. Recommendations for tenure must be made early in the school year so that any person eligible for tenure will know before the first of the year whether it has been granted to him. He might want to seek another position. The administrative procedure is set in motion by a memo to the department heads to have representatives elected for the Tenure Committee.

LESSON 59

59-A. System Control

This article contains 150 standard words. Your instructor will preview it and then dictate it until you can record it easily in one minute.

59-B. THE OFFICE: A Decision-Making Center

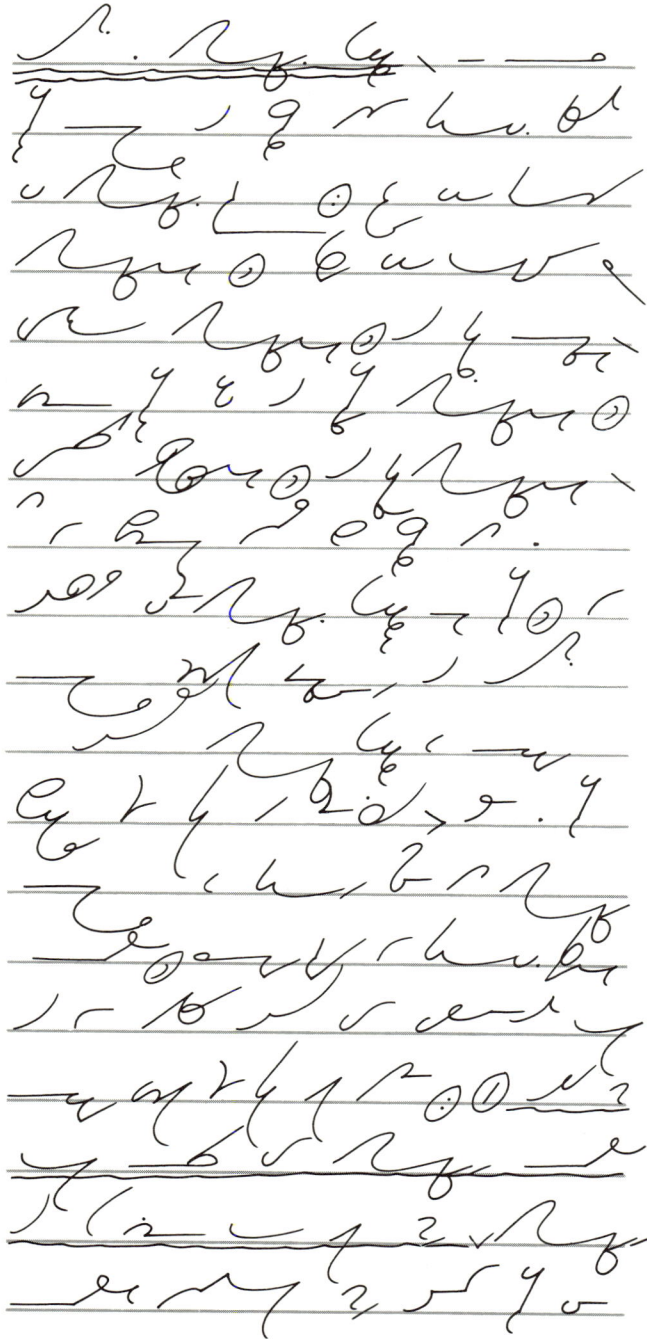

BACKGROUND FOR COMMUNICATION #2. The institution has in its budget funds for sabbatical leave for faculty for professional development. This memo to the faculty reminds them of the deadline for submitting applications.

BACKGROUND FOR COMMUNICATION #3. The college is celebrating its 50th Anniversary; and it is writing to its alumni, detailing events for Homecoming Weekend and urging them to be present for the festivities.

Golden, Anniversary, observance, graduated, Homecoming, Blackstone, orchestra, gala, reunite

BACKGROUND FOR COMMUNICATION #4. The Chairman of the Education Department has recently become aware of the fact that no course of study is available which specifically provides for presentation of the Four Cardinal Principles of Education. He suggests that the four Principles be discussed in History and Philosophy of Education classes. This memo will be dictated in office style.

58-D. Proofreading Exercise

The following letter contains 35 errors in grammar, spelling, punctuation, word division, word choice, letter style, consistency, or typewriting. Type a copy of the letter as it appears in this exercise; then edit your typed copy, making the necessary corrections in pen or pencil. Begin the date on line 12 and leave a one-inch left margin.

Aug. 1, 19--

Mr. J. Carter Dawson Jr., Manager
KWII Television Station
1 South Upland Road
Seattle, WN 98118

Dear Mr. Carter:

    The IBS network is announcing certain changes in its Fall evening programming schedule. You will need to be aware of these changes as you plan your local schedule for the coming season.

The following network programs are being dropped; The Sunday Evening Concert Hour, Jack Taylor's Amature Show, Lone Star Ranch, The Carter Comedy Hour, Nancy's Neighbors, and Its Happening.

The new shows schedulled for the coming season includes: Like Groovy!, Thursday at 7:30 p.m.; Weekly News Analysis, Friday at 10:30 a.m., Heritage House, Wednesday at 9 p.m.; and Sunday Theater, Sunday at 9 p.m..

Local networks will have open time for syndicated and-or local broadcasts from 7 to 8:30 p.m. on Monday, Wednesday, and Friday of each week. On Tuesday's and Thursday's they will have open time from 9:00 p.m. until sign off. Times are subject to change when television specials are aired.

The evening schedule for returning shows will remain substantialy the same. The net work may make some last minute changes which will be announced no latter than September 15th.

The network solicits the reactions and suggestions of your staff and you viewers concerning our fall programing. We are anticipating and exciting viewing season with a variety of programs to meet the interests of a broad-range of viewers. Our perodic rating survays will resume in October.

                                        Cordialy yours,

                                        Eldon P. Sites, Vice Pres.

sn

LESSON 14

14-A. Effective Display Guidelines

PAPER—THE "CARRIER" OF COMMUNICATIONS. Manifold paper, i.e., lightweight paper used for file copies and for extra carbon copies is available in different sizes, weights, qualities, finishes, color, and grain.

The most commonly used size is 8½ by 11 inches; but other sizes are also available. In fact, the paper can be cut to any size just as paper for original copies can.

The most frequently used weight of manifold paper is 9-pound. Other weights include 8-, 13-, and 16-pound.

Manifold paper may be manufactured entirely from wood pulp, entirely from cotton fibers, or from a combination of wood pulp and cotton fibers. Manifold paper made entirely from cotton fibers is called "onionskin."

If manifold paper is used that has both a dull and a glossy, or glazed side, the typing should be done on the dull side.

Color is used more often for carbon copies than it is used for originals in extraoffice correspondence. Many different colors are available for purchase, such as yellow, blue, green, buff, pink, and salmon. Color in file copies can facilitate filing and finding if a specific color is assigned to each department, such as yellow for the Advertising Department and blue for the Payroll Department.

Precollated sets are used by some firms for at least part of their typescripts. These sets are copy sheets with one-time carbon attached. These sets, while somewhat more expensive than unassembled sheets and carbon paper, save assembly time and insure sharp imprints.

Carbon paper varies in quality, weight, color, and size. The most frequently used size is, as would be expected, one suitable for 8½ by 11 inch stationery. Black is the color most frequently used, but some colors such as red are useful for effecting emphasis of certain facts or figures.

The better the quality of carbon, the harder the surface coating of carbon, thus reducing the problem of smudges and roller marks.

The greater the number of copies to be made the lighter the weight of carbon that should be used in order to reduce the thickness of the carbon pack, thus insuring maximum sharpness of impression on the last copy.

Carbon paper that is slightly longer than the stationery and that has the top left and bottom right corners cut facilitates disassembly of a pack. The secretary can grasp the upper left corners of the stationery and the lower right edges of the carbon sheets and then disassemble in one motion. This procedure minimizes handling the carbon sheets and reduces the likelihood of dirty fingers. Having both the corners cut also permits reversing the carbon sheets vertically to get maximum usage.

Another type of carbon paper that is available has a vertical line scale in the form of a strip that extends down the right edge of the carbon sheet. It extends beyond the stationery so that the secretary can ascertain on which line she is typing.

14-B. Transcription Craftsmanship

BASIC TECHNIQUES FOR ERROR CORRECTION. Even the master typist will make an error occasionally. If the correction is expertly made, the reader will not be aware of it. Since attractive appearance of a typescript promotes that important good first impression, acquiring skill in error correction is well worth the effort involved in the acquisition. The basic steps to be used in this process, appear on the following page:

Background: Mr. Bricker, Chief of Recruitment for the U. S. Civil Service, is authorizing the Miller Advertising Agency to begin work on a recruitment project. Send a carbon copy of this letter to J. P. Mahaffey, Director, U. S. Civil Service. The reply reference code is CSRT-21-4. Send the letter airmail.

disseminate, commercials, promotional, careers, factual, occupational, abroad, announcements, scripts, imagination, reproduced, tentatively

Letter 3
(to be dictated)

Dictator: John P. McNary, Chief

Addressee: Mr. Fred C. Biehle, Postmaster, U. S. Post Office, Denver, CO 80201

Background: Mr. McNary, Chief of the Postal Rate Commission, is reminding postmasters to notify commercial mailers of the forthcoming rise in third-class postage rates. The reference code is PRCR-33-9. Send a carbon copy of this letter to: Director, U. S. Postal Service. Send the letter airmail.

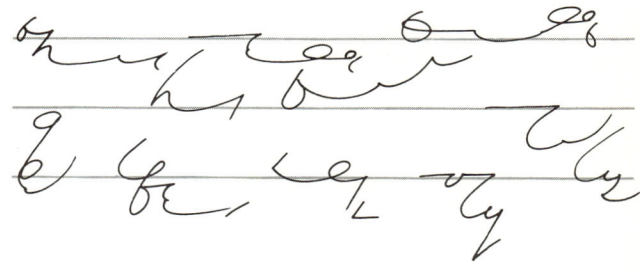

circulars, miscellaneous, simultaneously, bulk, calendar, imprint, adjacent, precanceled, clarification, nonprofit, brochure

Letter 2
(to be dictated)

Dictator: Paul F. Bricker, Chief

Addressee: Mr. S. T. Miller, Miller Advertising Agency, 224 Broadway, New York, NY 10007

1. Depress the margin release key and move the carriage to one side so the eraser crumbs will not fall into the machine. If the error is on the right half of the page, move the carriage to the right; if it is on the left half, move the carriage to the left. If a Selectric is used, move the typing element so that the eraser crumbs will not fall onto it.

2. Erase the error with light strokes; do not scrub. Brush crumbs away from the machine. If you have a new ribbon or a carbon ribbon, plastic type cleaner or kneaded rubber should be used to take off most of the ink impression before you use the eraser. Use of the type cleaner will prevent any smudges on the paper and will eliminate the problem of black carbon streaks on the eraser. An eraser shield or a 5 x 3 card may be used to protect letters adjacent to the error.

3. Type the correct letter or letters, being careful not to use too much force. If an electric typewriter is being used, the touch control can be adjusted to a lighter stroke and then returned to its normal position.

Here are the basic steps for multiple-copy erasing and correcting:

1. Move the carriage, depressing margin release key to go to the extreme left or right as needed.

2. Place a 5 x 3 card between the original and carbon copy while the original is being erased. Do not put the card behind the carbon sheet. If you do, pressure of erasing will remove the carbon surface and reduce the life of the carbon paper.

3. Remove as much ink as possible with plastic type cleaner; then erase with light strokes of a typing eraser.

4. Remove the card and place it between the first carbon sheet and the first carbon copy to form a "trough" to catch eraser crumbs. If more than one carbon copy is in the machine, put a second card immediately behind the first carbon copy to protect the other copies. Again, remove as much of the carbon impression as possible with plastic cleaner; then erase with a soft eraser.

5. Hold card firmly against the copy and flick out eraser crumbs. Blow out any crumbs that remain.

6. Position the carriage to the proper point and type correct letter or letters.

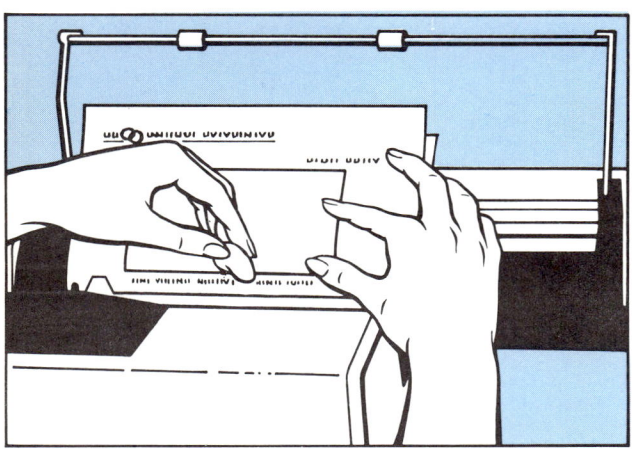

single space below the symbol cc:. This information does *not* appear on the *original* copy. (When you are ready to type the carbon copy notation, roll the platen toward you an appropriate distance, insert a sheet of translucent paper behind the carbon pack, return the platen to the typing point, and type the notation on the inserted sheet. The notation will then appear on the carbon copies only.)

▶ **58-C. Transcription Letters**

Follow the government style for the letters in this lesson. Use modified block and mixed punctuation.

Letter 1

Dictator: Arnold A. Garber, Administrative Assistant, Federal Communications Commission

Addressee: Dr. C. J. Simpson, Department of Communication, Bowling Green State University, Bowling Green, OH 43402

Background: Mr. Garber has the responsibility of lining up expert witnesses for a forthcoming Senate subcommittee hearing on television programming. Send a carbon copy of this letter to Senator James L. Spring, Chairman, Subcommittee on Television. The reply reference code is SSTV-30-2. Send the letter airmail.

7. The reference initials include the writer's first initial and surname, a colon, the typist's initials, and the date. This information does not appear on the original copy. To exclude this information on the original copy, use the same procedure as described in No. 6.

8. One-inch side and bottom margins are usually used in government correspondence.

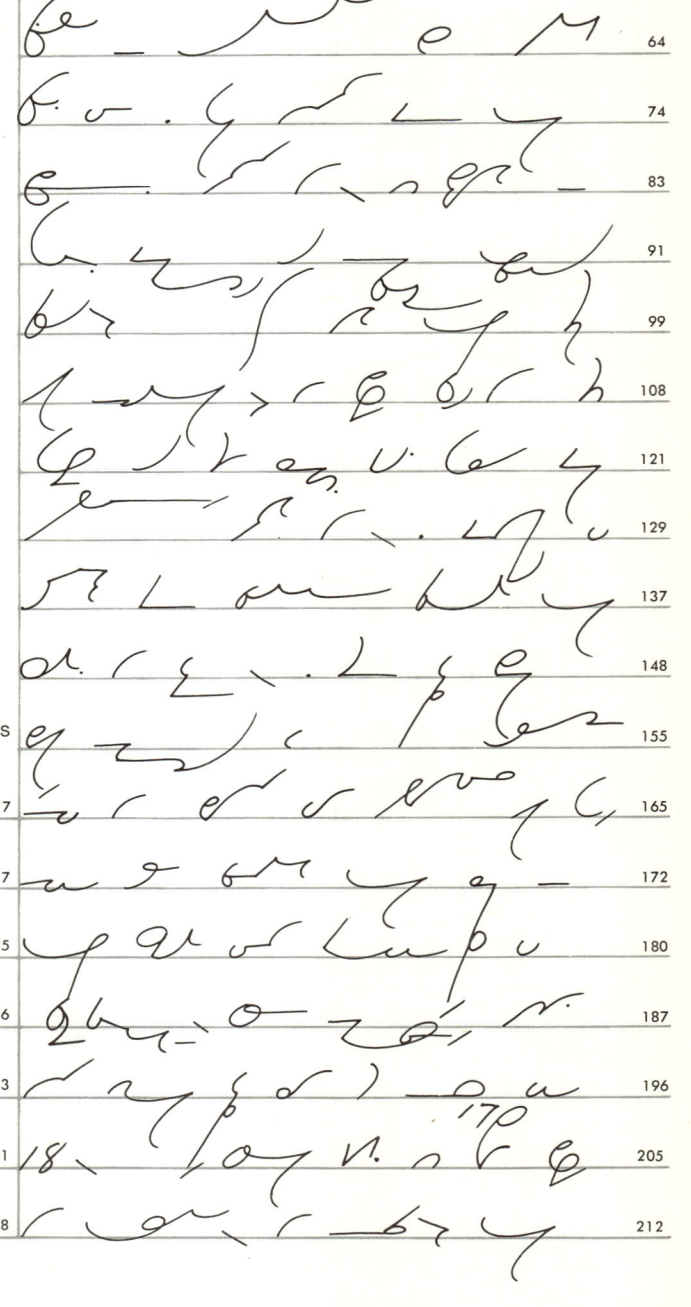

14-C. Communication in Education

BACKGROUND FOR COMMUNICATION #2. This bulletin contains the first of the four major educational objectives referred to in Communication #4 in 13-D.

DIRECTIONS TO THE TRANSCRIBER. The statement of objectives will be duplicated, so no carbon copy is required. Use 8½ by 11 bond paper. Center the heading BULLETIN #2, on the 15th line from the top of the page. Double space to the subheading, and center it. Type in initial caps and underscore. Triple-space to the body. Use a 60-space line. Indent the lettered items 5 spaces from the left margin and double space between the items.

14-D. Transcription Capsules

The other three educational objectives are explained. Use the same machine setup as for 14-C. Read in thought phrases.

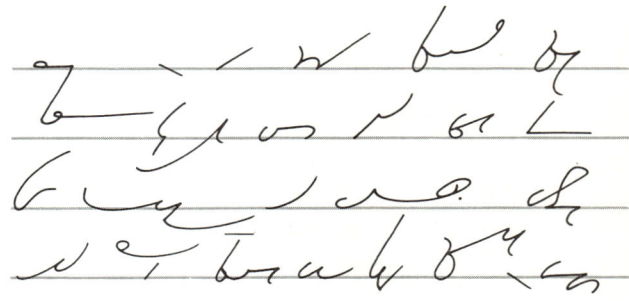

Letter 2
(Office-Style Dictation)

Dictator: T. L. Poole, Advertising Manager

Addressee: Mr. Frederick Cooper, President, Ade Bottling Company, 2094 Main Street, Bridgeport, CT 06606

Background: Mr. Poole is soliciting a sponsor for the new TV show, "The Public Wants to Know."

LESSON 58

58-A. Special Problems

FEDERAL GOVERNMENT CORRESPONDENCE. Government correspondence is prepared on 8″ x 10½″ letterhead. No. 9 envelopes are used with this stationery. Window envelopes are frequently used. Special reference lines are used in government correspondence to indicate both the sender's and the addressee's identifying codes, symbols, or the subject of the message.

58-B. Transcription Craftsmanship

TIPS ON TYPING GOVERNMENT CORRESPONDENCE. A model letter that illustrates the government correspondence style appears on page vii in the Appendix. Special attention should be given to these points, which differ from nongovernment correspondence:

1. The date line is typed a double space below the letterhead. It is begun 2½ inches from the right edge of the paper.

2. The reference lines are also begun 2½ inches from the right edge of the paper and are typed a double space below the date line. The lines are single spaced and separated by a double space.

3. The special mailing instructions are typed on line 12, a double space above the inside address.

4. The inside address is begun on line 14 so that the address will be in the proper position for a window envelope.

5. The items to be enclosed with the letter are listed a single space below the word *Enclosure*. Underscore the titles of any publications which appear in the list.

6. The names and titles of the individuals to receive carbon copies are listed a

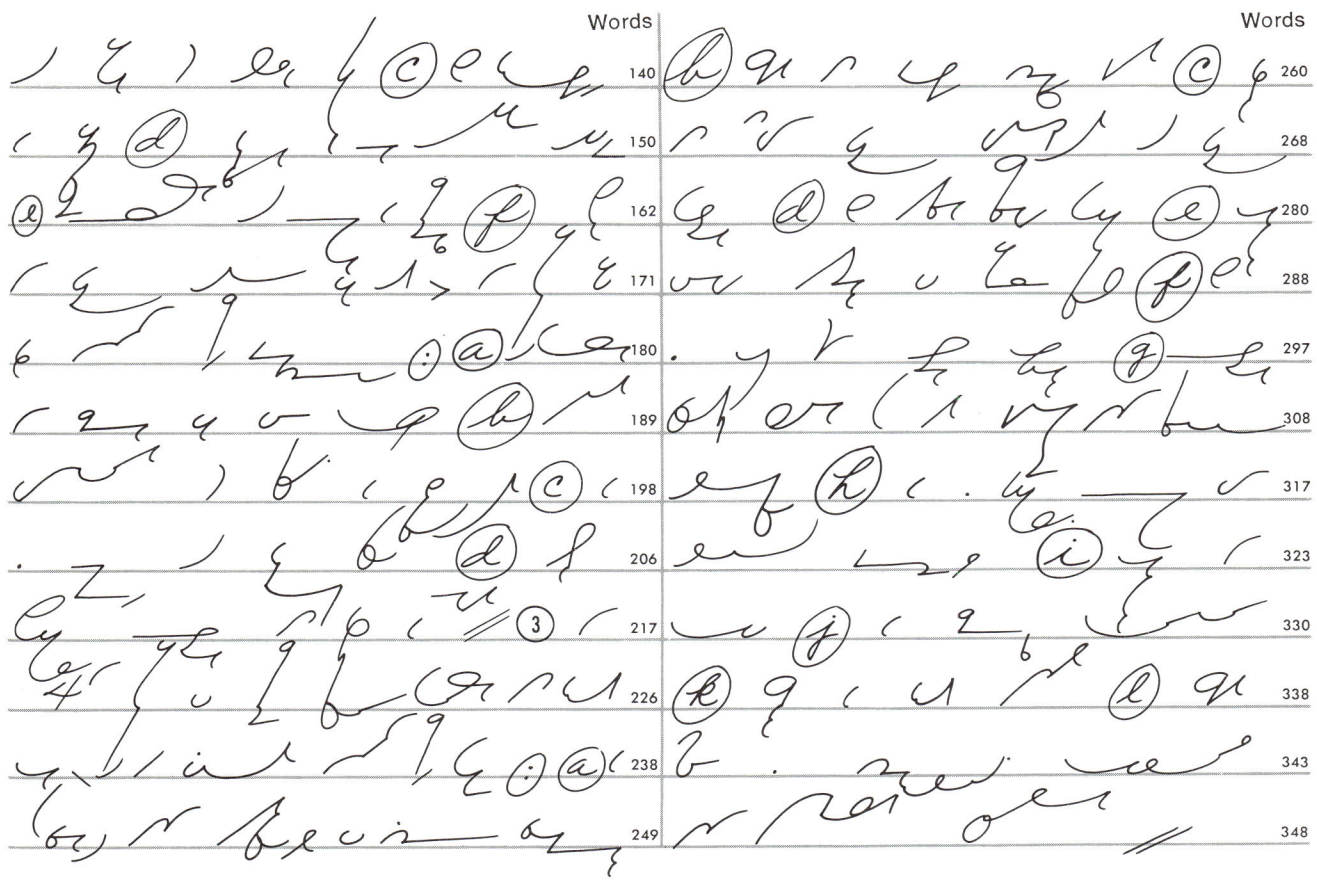

LESSON 15

15-A. System Control

The shorthand notes below provide for automatization of five phrases beginning with *it will*.

15-B. THE OFFICE: A Decision-Making Center

57-C. Executive Language in Mass Media

open-circuit broadcasts (ō′ pən sėr′ kit brôd′ kasts′), n. television broadcasts that are transmitted by means of electromagnetic radiation.

coaxial cable (kō ak′ sē əl kā′ bl), n. a connecting cable containing an insulated conductor that is used for transmitting television impulses.

grid (grid), n. a network of wires.

57-D. Communication in Mass Media

Letter 1

Dictator: Roger L. Bennett, Manager

Addressee: Mrs. Terry Stevens, Box 616, LaCrosse, KS 67548

Background: Mr. Bennett is explaining to Mrs. Stevens why his company cannot extend cable service to her new home.

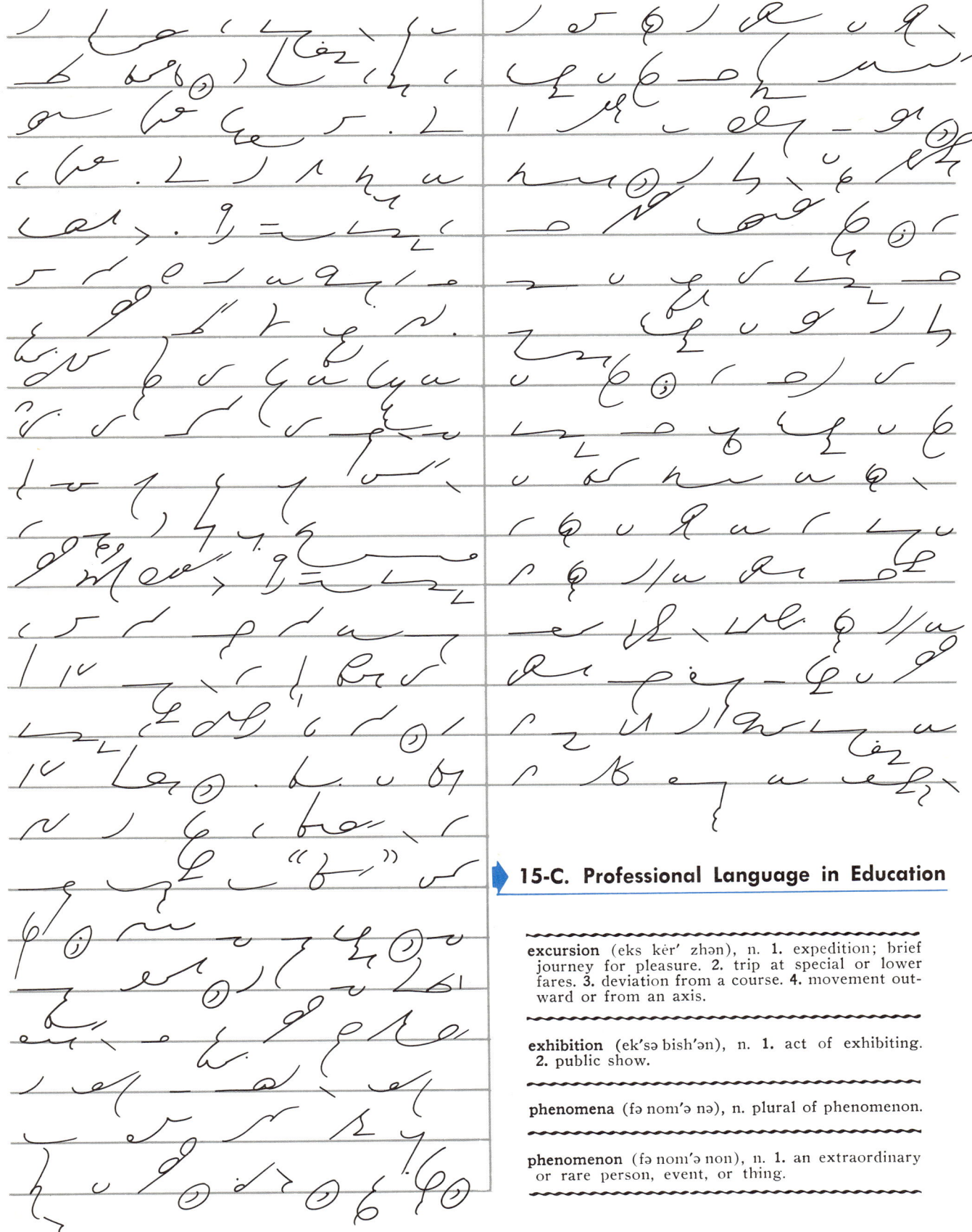

15-C. Professional Language in Education

excursion (eks kėr′ zhən), n. 1. expedition; brief journey for pleasure. 2. trip at special or lower fares. 3. deviation from a course. 4. movement outward or from an axis.

exhibition (ek′sə bish′ən), n. 1. act of exhibiting. 2. public show.

phenomena (fə nom′ə nə), n. plural of phenomenon.

phenomenon (fə nom′ə non), n. 1. an extraordinary or rare person, event, or thing.

15-D. Communication in Education

BACKGROUND FOR COMMUNICATION #1. The art classes sponsored last year by the Art Department were so successful that they are being repeated this year. This memo is the announcement.

BACKGROUND FOR COMMUNICATION #2. The School of Speech and Theater Arts has planned a series of telelectures on the frontiers of speech communication during the school year. This memo announces the plan and schedule.

attendance, behavioral, universal, phenomenon, awaken, sensitivities, perspective, frontiers, dynamic, conceptual, telelectures, studios, videotaped

57-A. System Control

This exercise, dealing with the validation of advertising claims, contains 150 standard words. Your instructor will preview the article and then dictate it until you can record it in one minute.

57-B. THE OFFICE: A Decision-Making Center

LESSON 16

16-A. System Control

Note the phrases beginning with *I will*.

16-B. THE OFFICE: A Decision-Making Center

UNIT 3 COMMUNICATION IN MANUFACTURING

56-D. Proofreading Exercise

The following letter contains 35 errors in grammar, spelling, punctuation, word division, word choice, letter style, consistency, or typewriting. Type a copy of the letter as it appears in this exercise; then edit your typed copy, making the necessary corrections in pen or pencil. Begin the date on line 12 and leave a one-inch left margin.

June 22, 19--

Miss Wanda James
1712 Blaine Ave.
Terrehaute, IN 47804

Dear Ms. James:

You have asked why your letter to the editor dated June 16 was not published in The Evening Herald. You may be insured that carefull attention was given to your letter. While we may not always agree with the opinions expressed in letters submitted for our "Letters To The Editor" column, we do print them if they do not violate one or more of the rules that has been extablished for such letters. These rules which appear at the end of the column everyday are as follows.

1. Letters are not to accede 250 words in length.

2. All letters must he signed. (A writers name will be witheld from the column at their request.

3. An individual's complete address must appear on his letter.

4. Obscene words and affensive terminology will not be printed.

5. At his discretion, the editor may refrain from printing a letter. Some letters may contain information that is quite similiar to that which appears in letters from other correspondants. Some times letters may not be of general interest to the public.

Your letter was not printed because you did not include you name and address on it. Your letter contained some excellent points about the up-coming city election. If you wish to resubmit you're letter with the necessary signature and address, we will probably be able to print it.

Sincerely Yours

Theodore L. Updyke, editor

P. S. If you do not wish to have your name appear in the column please indicate this fact at the bottom of your letter.

sm

Record of a Long-Distance Call

Record of a Local Call

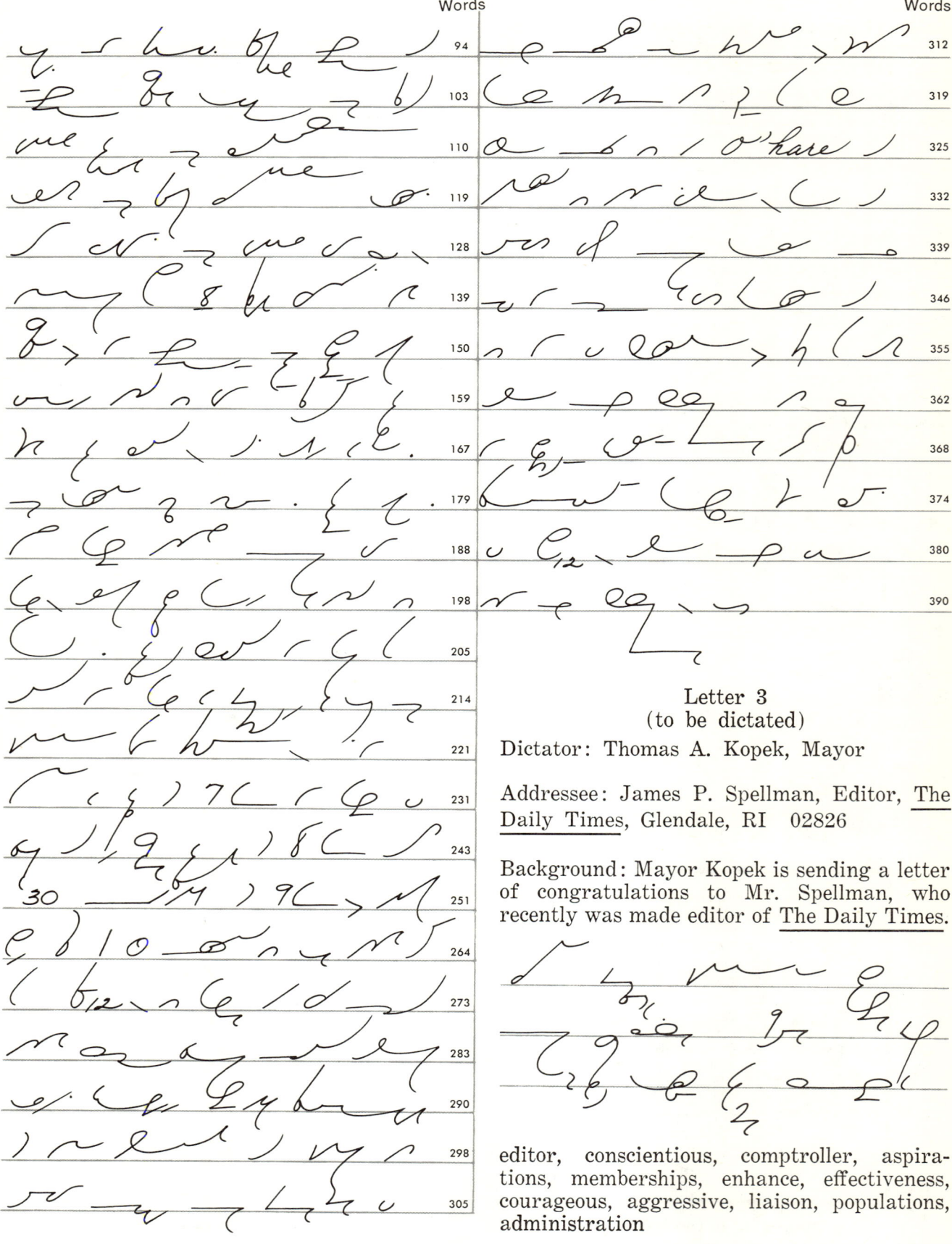

Letter 3
(to be dictated)

Dictator: Thomas A. Kopek, Mayor

Addressee: James P. Spellman, Editor, The Daily Times, Glendale, RI 02826

Background: Mayor Kopek is sending a letter of congratulations to Mr. Spellman, who recently was made editor of The Daily Times.

editor, conscientious, comptroller, aspirations, memberships, enhance, effectiveness, courageous, aggressive, liaison, populations, administration

16-C. Executive Language in Manufacturing

accountability (ə koun′tə bil′ə tē), n. quality of being accountable.

maximization (mak səm ə zāshən), n. act of maximizing.

prudence (prüd′ns), n. 1. ability to govern oneself by reason or good judgment. 2. discretion in the management of affairs, or resources; economy.

16-D. Communication in Manufacturing

BACKGROUND FOR COMMUNICATION #1. The Executive Vice President in Charge of Sales has decided to send to the managers, in the Home Office and the Branch Offices, a statement of factors to be considered by them in evaluating the effectiveness of the sales representatives under their supervision.

Letter 2

Dictator: B. T. Kendrick, Vice-President

Addressee: Governor Alton S. Page, State Capitol Complex, Springfield, IL 62706

Background: Mr. Kendrick, Vice-President of the National Newspaper Association, is extending an invitation to Governor Page to speak at the annual awards banquet.

BACKGROUND FOR COMMUNICATION #2. Another memo is sent about the factors for evaluating effectiveness of representatives.

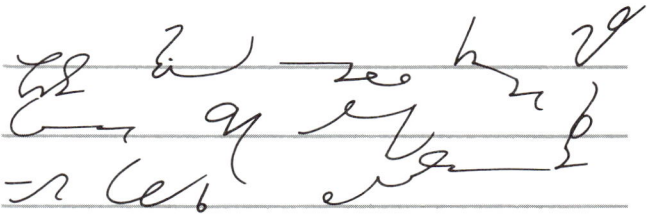

reputation, uphold, missionary, functions, update, promptness, accountable, intelligent, fraction, interviews, periodically, entertainment

BACKGROUND FOR COMMUNICATION #3. The Executive Vice President's statement is concluded in this third memo of the series. This memo will be dictated in office style.

LESSON 17

17-A. Effective Display Guidelines

READABILITY FACTORS. Various factors contribute to the readability of a typewritten communication. Some of the primary objectives which readability depends upon are listed below:

type style	space "breaks"
type size	ribbon quality
arrangement of copy	ribbon color

There are many different type styles which are available for typewriters. The four basic type faces used in printing are generally known as Text, Roman, Italic, and Script:

𝔗𝔥𝔦𝔰 𝔦𝔰 𝔰𝔢𝔱 𝔦𝔫 𝔱𝔢𝔵𝔱.

This is set in roman.

This is set in italics.

This is set in script.

Distinct classes of letter forms may be identified as: Old Style, Modern, Sans Serif, Square Serif, Text, Script. There are variations in thickness or thinness of strokes, in presence or absence of serifs

LESSON 56

56-A. Special Problem

OFFICIAL OR INFORMAL LETTER STYLE. The official or informal letter style is sometimes used when a business letter is sent to a distinguished official or when the message is of a semipersonal nature, such as a letter of appreciation, condolence, or congratulations. Some feel that the unique position of the inside address gives the letter a more prestigious or personal look. To carry out the distinctive appearance in a letter of this kind, the secretary often uses a smaller size of letterhead, which may be called monarch or executive stationery. It usually measures 7¼" by 10½".

56-B. Transcription Craftsmanship

TIPS FOR TYPING THE OFFICIAL OR INFORMAL LETTER STYLE ON 7¼" BY 10½" STATIONERY. The inside address is placed at the left margin, below the closing lines of the business letter, when the official or informal style is used. Other parts of the letter are typed according to the letter and punctuation style preferred. A commonly used style appears on page vii in the Appendix.

When typing a letter on 7¼" by 10½" stationery, one must keep in mind these three facts as he determines his margins and arranges his copy: (1) there are 87 elite spaces or 73 pica spaces available on a horizontal line, (2) the elite centering point is 43 and the pica centering point is 36, and (3) there are 63 vertical lines available on the sheet.

56-C. Transcription Letters

Use the official or informal letter style illustrated on page vii in the Appendix for the letters in this lesson. Type them on 7¼" by 10½" letterhead.

Letter 1

Dictator: Janice Halvorson, Office Manager

Addressee: Mrs. T. L. Andrews, 115 Seubert Avenue, Sioux Falls, SD 57104

Background: Mrs. Halvorson is writing a letter of condolence to a stenographer in the News Bureau whose son just died.

UNIT 11 COMMUNICATION IN MASS MEDIA

at ends of letters, and in boldness (darkness) of imprint. Letters also differ in width, with some condensed and others expanded:

Old Style	Sans Serif
Modern	**Square Serif**
Script	Text

The type size selected may affect readability. Students in transcription classes are most likely to be familiar with *pica* and *elite*, but other sizes are available for typewriters:

```
This is pica.
```

```
This is elite.
```

Space "breaks" also promote readability. Double-spaced copy is easier to read than single-spaced because of the greater amount of "white" space. Spacing between paragraphs increases the readability as does indention for paragraphs.

Generous margins at the left, right, and bottom of the typed material contribute to greater readability. The traditional practice of leaving at least one inch for margins arose out of the need for "space breaks."

Ribbon quality is a factor in readability. One-time ribbons produce an evenness of impression not possible with a used fabric ribbon. Silk or nylon ribbons tend to produce more attractive copy than cotton because the letters print with finer lines. Heavily-inked ribbons produce "thicker" imprints than do medium-inked ribbons. Ribbons other than black are available, but generally speaking, they do not provide the "mileage" of clear imprints that is provided by black.

Arrangement of copy can enhance readability of typed copy through the judicious use of listings, marginal headings, and paragraph headings illustrated on this page.

**Minutes of a Meeting
(with marginal headings)**

**Minutes of a Meeting
(with paragraph headings)**

**Excerpt from a Report
(with listing)**

55-D. Proofreading Exercise

The following letter contains 35 errors in grammar, spelling, punctuation, word division, word choice, consistency, letter style or typewriting. Type a copy of the material as it appears below; then edit your typed copy, making the necessary corrections in pen or pencil. Begin the date on line 12 and use a 1-inch left margin.

August 1, 19--

Daniel Taylor
901 Grand St.
Bryan, OH 43506

SUBJECT: Recreation Vehicles

Dear Mr. Daniel Taylor:

The production of vacation vehicles is becoming one of the most rapidly-growing industrys in the United States, furthermore, it is becoming one of the Nations' most popular past times. It is estimated that there are 3.5 million recreation vehicles in use. In a decade this figure is expected to raise to 7,500,000.

The pickup cover is the basic recreational vehicle. It is a portable unit which is priced anywhere from $200 to $1,000. It is placed on the bed of a pickup truck. It is often used by sports men for shelter add has limited facilitys.

The camping trailer has also become quiet popular. It is a compack unit and can be folded down for towing. When it is prepared for us as a sleeping unit it springs out in several directions. Prices range from $300 to $2,500.

Then there is the truck camper, which is designed to be carried on one half ton or larger trucks. This unit is designed for family-use and is much more roomier and comfortably equiped then the pickup cover. The truck camper may range in price from $1,000 to $10,000, depending upon the degree of luxury desired.

A more luxurious recreation vehicle is the travel trailer, which may range up to thirty five feet in length. This vehicle is designed to be towed behind a passenger car, and often is a selfcontained living unit. Some of these vehicles costs as much as $18000.

The elete member of the recreation-vehicle family is the motor home. In such a vehicle the driver appears to be driving from the livingroom. This vehicle is not towed for it has it's own engine. It too, can have luxurious appointments. The most elegant motor homes sell for more than $20,000.

Why not visit our display. Details are given in the enclosed brochure.

Sincerely,

Terry Kelly, Agent

jb

17-B. Transcription Craftsmanship

SQUEEZING AND SPREADING IN ERROR CORRECTION. Sometimes the correction of an error requires an extra letter be squeezed in or one less letter be used in the space that was taken for the word containing the error.

To insert a word in a space smaller than it normally occupies, use the technique illustrated in changing "herd" to "heard."

I herd the rumor.

1. Erase the word "herd."
2. Move carriage pointer to space preceding the position of "h" in "herd." Depress space bar and strike "h." Release space bar and depress again. Type "e." Proceed in a similar manner to type each of the remaining letters.

I heard the rumor.

To insert a word in a space larger than it normally occupies, use the technique illustrated in changing "needed" to "needs."

He needed a new desk.

1. Erase the word "needed."
2. Move carriage pointer to space formerly occupied by "n." Depress space bar and strike "n." Release space bar and depress it again. Type "e." Proceed in a similar manner for each remaining letter.

He needs a new desk.

NOTE: To spread or squeeze letters on an electric typewriter, hold the carriage at the right spot with one hand while striking the correct key with the other, except on machines that have a half-space key.

17-C. Communication in Manufacturing

BACKGROUND FOR COMMUNICATION #3. This bulletin contains a list of rules for reducing pilferage in the manufacturing plant.

DIRECTIONS TO THE TRANSCRIBER. An original and a carbon copy are required. Center the heading, BULLETIN #3, on the 21st line from the top of the page. Double space to the subheading and triple space from the subheading to the first item. Use a 70-space line. Double space between items. Make an effort to read in thought phrases.

Lesson 55

Page 173

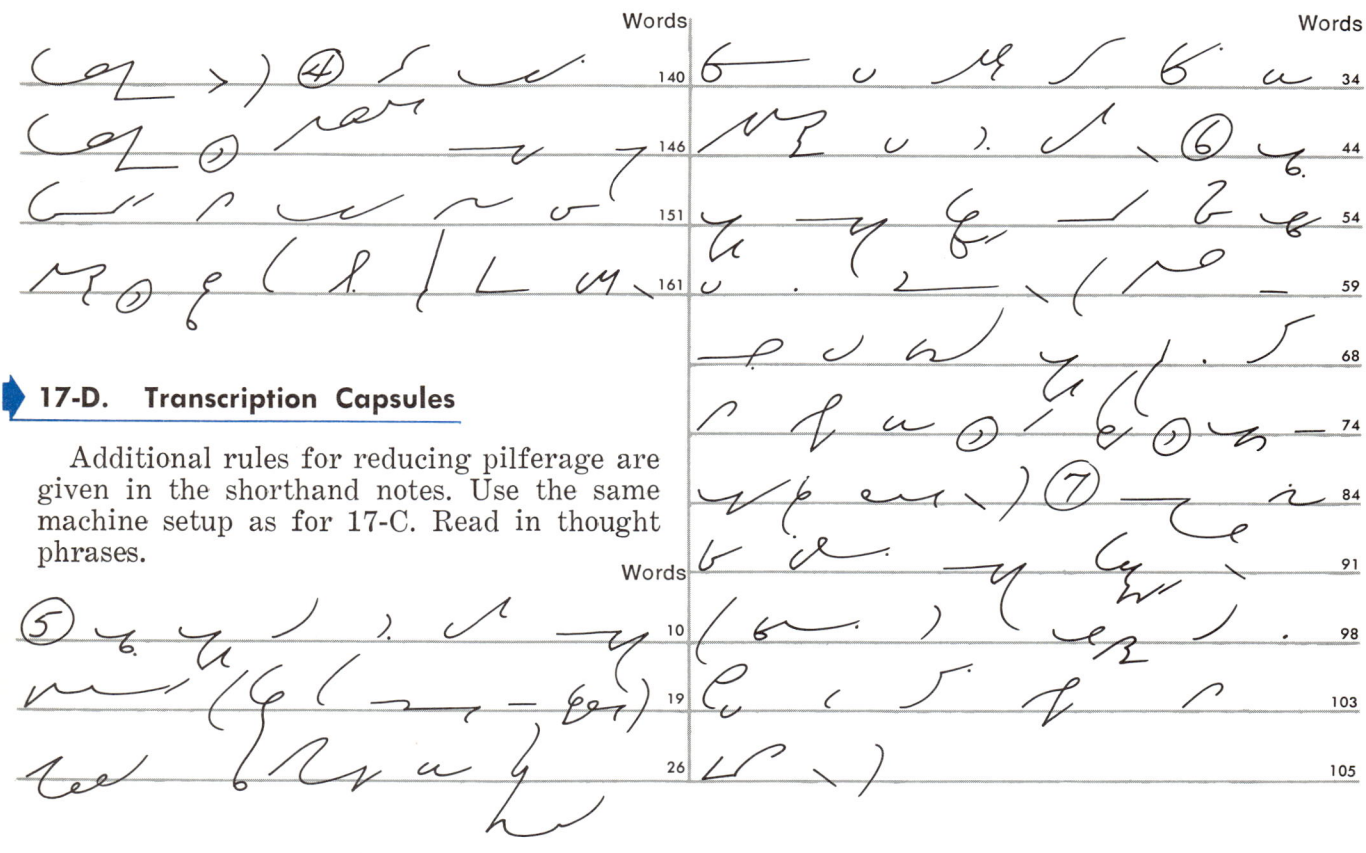

17-D. Transcription Capsules

Additional rules for reducing pilferage are given in the shorthand notes. Use the same machine setup as for 17-C. Read in thought phrases.

LESSON 18

18-A. System Control

The shorthand notes provide for automatization of some phrases beginning with *you may*.

18-B. THE OFFICE: A Decision-Making Center

55-C. Transcription Letter

Use the AMS Simplified Letter style, which is illustrated on page vii in the Appendix, with two modifications: (1) omit the subject line, and (2) use the traditional closing lines. This modified style is used by some firms. Use the appropriate second-page heading.

Dictator: Robert Smart, Vice President

Addressee: Roy Harris, 1202 Rylie Road, Dallas, TX 75217

Background: Mr. Smart is explaining to a policyholder why car insurance premiums for young drivers are so high.

Letter 2
(Office-Style Dictation)

Dictator: Daniel Short, Public Relations Director

Addressee: Miss Catherine Jones, Manager, Jones Employment Service, Box 1292, Jackson, MI 49204

Background: Mr. Short is notifying travel bureaus about forthcoming AMTRAK sleeping car routes.

passenger, AMTRAK, network, localities, billeting, transcontinental, Union, complimentary, previously, consistently, families

▶▶▶ LESSON 55 ◀◀◀

▶ 55-A. Special Problems

HEADINGS FOR MULTIPAGE LETTERS. A letter of more than one page must carry a distinct heading on the second and succeeding pages. This heading should contain three elements: (1) the first line of the inside address, (2) the page number, and (3) the date of the letter. The addressee's name and the date will identify the letter to which the page belongs if it inadvertently becomes separated from the letter. The page number indicates the order in which the pages should be assembled.

▶ 55-B. Transcription Craftsmanship

TIPS ON TYPING HEADINGS FOR MULTIPAGE LETTERS. The second and any succeeding pages of a letter should be typed on plain paper that matches the letterhead stationery that is used for the first page. A word should never be divided between two pages of a letter. At least two lines of a paragraph should appear at both the bottom and the top of each page of a multipage letter. The heading for the second page and each remaining page of a multipage letter is begun approximately one inch from the top of the paper. It is followed by a triple space. Examples of acceptable multipage letter headings are illustrated on page iv in the Appendix.

18-C. Executive Language in Manufacturing

divest (də vest'), v. 1. to take away from a person; rid, free. 2. to undress or strip. 3. to deprive of title, authority, or property.

docket (dok' it), n. 1. brief summary of a document. 2. list of legal causes to be tried; record of proceedings in a legal action; agenda. 3. label giving contents of a document. v. 1. to enter on a docket. 2. to make a summary.

stay (sta), v. 1. to stop going forward; halt. 2. stop or cease doing something. 3. put an end to; satisfy. 4. hold back; restrain. 5. endure. 6. live for awhile; dwell in the same place.

18-D. Communication in Manufacturing

BACKGROUND FOR COMMUNICATION #1. This letter is the first of three from a jewelry manufacturing firm to its patrons regarding a decision of the Federal Trade Commission ordering the parent company to divest itself of interest in that firm.

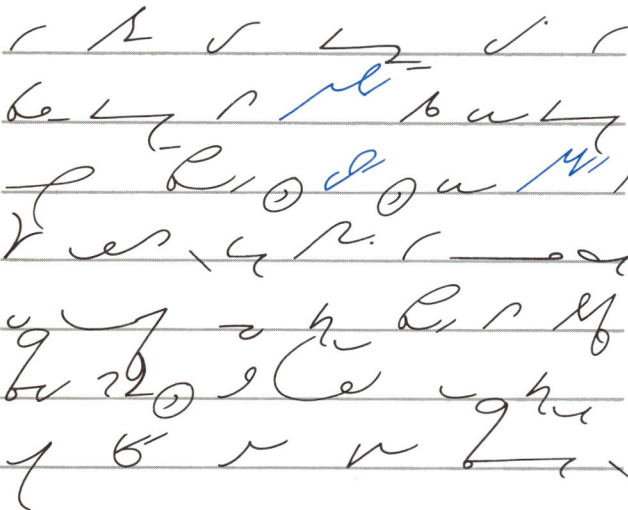

BACKGROUND FOR COMMUNICATION #2. This letter gives additional information regarding the FTC decision.

adverse, circulation, fraternity, insignia, sororities, equivalent, litigation, testify, obvious, sanction, nullify.

BACKGROUND FOR COMMUNICATION #3. This letter responds to an inquiry as to whether the Donaldson and Vinson Company will continue to fill orders for jewelry as in the past. The communication will be dictated in office style.

54-C. Executive Language in Transportation

bidirectional (bī də rek′ shən l), adj. capable of moving in opposite directions.

AMTRAK (am′trak), n. a coined word derived from "American" and "track" to designate the U.S. railway system.

turbopowered (tér′ bō pou′ ərd), adj. powered by turbine engines.

54-D. Communication in Transportation

Letter 1

Dictator: J. P. Butcher, Senator from Montana

Addressee: James L. Gardiner, Governor, State Capitol, Helena, MT 59601

Background: The Senator is sending Governor Gardiner information about an experimental train that will pass through their state.

LESSON 19

19-A. Effective Display Guidelines

APPEARANCE FACTORS. The appearance of a transcript is a clue to the personal traits of the transcriber and to the character of the firm in which she works.

An attractively displayed message puts the recipient in a favorable frame of mind the instant he looks at it. Indirectly, the message says to him, "Your goodwill is important to us; we are putting our 'best foot' forward." It also says for the sending company, "We are proud of our product and of our business; we are genuinely interested in what we are doing." For both the transcriber and the firm it says, "We are careful, thoughtful people on whom you can depend."

One factor in attractive appearance is *balance*. If the imaginary line that could be drawn around the typed message is in proportion to the dimensions of the paper, the message will look "framed" as though it were a picture. Uneven left and right margins or a ragged right margin leaves an unattractive appearance. The popularity of a modified block letter style is probably partially due to its balanced appearance.

Unbalanced Transcript

Balanced Transcript

Another factor which a transcriber should consider in the attractive appearance of a finished transcript is the proper vertical placement of the typed message on the sheet of stationery. The *optical center* or **reading position**, as it is sometimes called, is about two line spaces above the *actual* or vertical center. In reality this means that the point which appears to the reader to be the center of the page is really two line spaces above the true center. For this reason, the bottom margin of the transcript needs to be slightly deeper than the top margin. Illustrations of transcripts showing both the optical and the actual centers are shown on the following page.

Lesson 19   Page 60

Transcript Using Optical Center

Still another factor in attractive appearance is the "clean look" of the transcript that comes from having been typed with clean keys. Clogged letters leave the same impression as dirty fingernails, unwashed hair, or wrinkled clothes. They reveal a lack of personal pride.

Transcript with Clogged Letters

Transcript Using Actual Center

Daily cleaning of the keys takes only a few seconds at the close of the day, but the resulting neat transcripts will leave an impression so favorable that it may generate months or years of confidence and goodwill.

Transcript with Clear Letters

19-B. Transcription Craftsmanship

CORRECTIONS ON CARBON COPIES. Carbon copies are typed in the expectation that they will be read by someone; they should be neat and easy to read. Corrections can be made on carbon copies in such a way that they are undetectable. Here are some suggested steps:

1. Move the carriage, depressing margin release key to go to extreme left or right as needed.

2. Place a 5 x 3 card between the original and carbon copy while the original is

LESSON 54

54-A. System Control

[shorthand notes]

54-B. THE OFFICE: A Decision-Making Center

[shorthand notes]

being erased. Do *not* put the card behind the carbon sheet. If you do, pressure of erasing will remove the carbon surface and reduce the life of the carbon paper.

3. Remove as much of the ink as possible with plastic type cleaner; erase with light strokes of a typing eraser.

4. Remove the card and place it between the first carbon sheet and the first carbon copy so as to form a "trough" to catch the eraser crumbs. If there is more than one carbon copy put a second card immediately behind the first carbon copy to protect the other copies. Again, remove as much of the carbon impression as possible with plastic cleaner; erase with a soft eraser.

5. Hold card firmly against the copy and flick out eraser crumbs. Blow out any remaining crumbs.

6. Position the carriage to the proper point and type the correction.

Special hints for making an undetectable correction:

1. Brush crumbs from original copy down toward the table; brush crumbs from carbon copies sideways from the machine. Crumbs that slip between the copies will prevent clear impressions in subsequent lines.

2. Always erase from the first to the last copy. In that way you will be sure that there are no smudges on any of the copies.

3. If papers have a tendency to slip when rolled forward or backward for erasing, hold them firmly against the platen as you turn the cylinder knob.

4. If the type is single spaced, a 5 x 3 card can be held over the line above the error or over adjacent letters to prevent erasing a letter that should not be disturbed.

5. Rub a punctuation mark on the back of the paper before erasing it.

6. To avoid a dark impression, strike the key lightly a few times if using a manual machine. If using an electric, adjust the touch control.

19-C. Communication in Manufacturing

BACKGROUND FOR COMMUNICATION #4. This bulletin is a second one issued regarding rules for controlling pilferage in the plant.

DIRECTIONS TO THE TRANSCRIBER. Follow the directions as for Bulletin #3 on page 56.

53-D. Proofreading Exercise

The letter on this page contains 35 errors in grammar, spelling, punctuation, word choice, consistency, letter style, or typewriting. Type a copy of the material as it appears in this exercise; then edit your typed copy, making the necessary corrections in pen or pencil. Begin on line 12 and leave a 1-inch left margin.

May 31, 19--

Mrs. Frank Koberstein
P. O. Box 613
Burchard, NE. 68323

Dear Mr. Koberstein

Perhaps you are one of the thousands of urban citizens who have taken to the bicycle-as a recreational out let, as a physical fitness aide, or simply as a means of non-polluting transportation. If you have decided to join your neighbors in the revival of this popular vehicle you will want to give careful consideration to a number of points before you purchase you bike.

How do you intend to use your bicycle? A bicycle used for a 30 minute daily exercize period need not be of the quality found in a $300.00 touring bike. On the other hand, the later is desirable if you plan to take a lengthy hostile trip. Remember, you will probably get just what you pay for.

Where should you purchase your bicycle? Shop around abit. Dont forget to check the classified adds for good used bikes. It may be wise to rent two or three types of bicycles that interest you most so that you can get the feel of them. Talk to a salesmen at you local bicycle shop. Ask him to show you the differances in the models on display.

What type of bicycle should you buy? The cyclist in an area with rolling terain such as our's will do well to get a bike of adequate size. He will want one with thin tires and a selection of at least three gears. The english-style bike with three or five speeds and hand-controlled breaks is adequate for normal use. The ten-speed bike is probably the most popular and versitile. It ranges in price any where from $60. to $300. You should be able to resale such a bicycle if you find your enthusiasm waining after a few weeks' of strenuous pedalling.

What size bicycle should you buy. The size of the frame is an important consideration when you select a bicycle. The frame should be large enough so that the seat may be raised sufficiently to permit almost a full extension of the leg when the ball of the foot is at the lowest point of the pedal swing.

Sincerly yours

H.D. Williams
Consumer Extention Agent

abp

19-D. Transcription Capsules

Additional rules for reducing pilferage are given. Follow the directions as for 19-C.

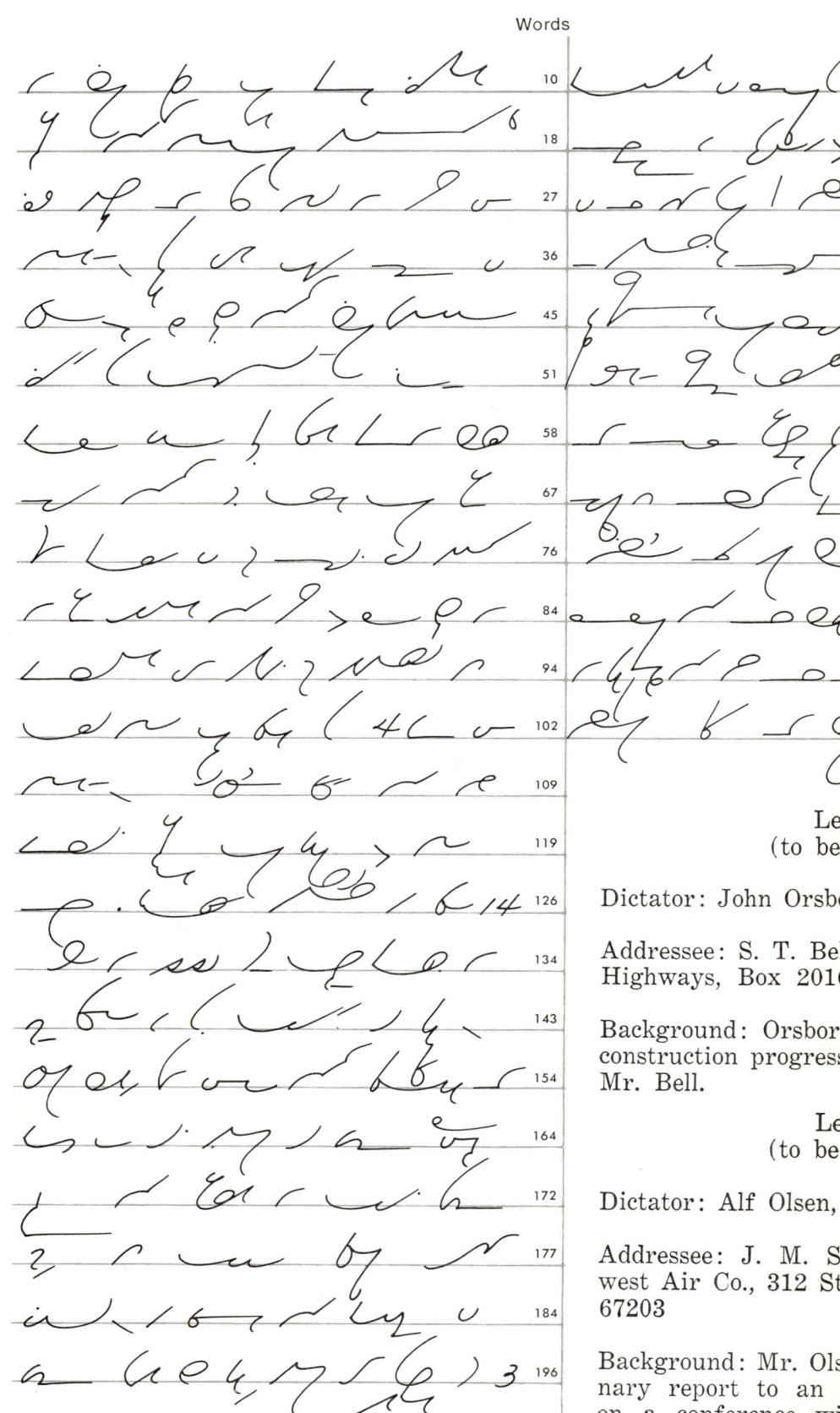

Letter 2
(to be dictated)

Dictator: John Orsborne, Highway Engineer

Addressee: S. T. Bell, Chief, Department of Highways, Box 2016, Olympia, WA 98501

Background: Orsborne is giving a highway construction progress report to his superior, Mr. Bell.

Letter 3
(to be dictated)

Dictator: Alf Olsen, Design Engineer

Addressee: J. M. Stevens, President, Midwest Air Co., 312 State Street, Wichita, KS 67203

Background: Mr. Olsen is sending a preliminary report to an official in his company on a conference with a renowned design engineer in Germany.

LESSON 20

20-A. System Control

Automatization of *if you* phrases is stressed in the notes.

20-B. THE OFFICE: A Decision-Making Center

LESSON 53

53-A. Signals in Written Communications

SUBJECT LINE. A subject line is used to orient the reader to the major topic that is presented in a piece of correspondence. The subject line may also serve as a convenient reference when one codes correspondence for subject filing.

53-B. Transcription Craftsmanship

TIPS ON TYPING SUBJECT LINE. In most business letters the subject line is typed a double space below the salutation. It may be typed at the left margin, typed at the paragraph point, or be centered. Three common subject-line styles appear below:

(1) SUBJECT: Approval of Secretarial Position

(2) Subject: Approval of Secretarial Position

(3) Approval of Secretarial Position (The word "Subject" is not used.)

The first word and all principal words of the subject are capitalized.

In the AMS Simplified Letter style the subject line is typed in all capital letters without the word "SUBJECT." It is placed a triple space below the inside address.

The first line of the body is begun a triple space below the subject line. (A salutation line is not used in the Simplified Letter style.)

In memorandums the subject line appears a double space below the "FROM:" line.

```
TO:         Office Manager

FROM:       Personnel Department

SUBJECT:    Approval of Secretarial Position
```

In military correspondence the subject line is typed at the left margin a double space below the reference symbol. This use of the subject line is illustrated below:

```
OM-PER

SUBJECT:    Approval of Secretarial Position
```

53-C. Transcription Letters

For the letters in this section use the AMS Simplified Letter style, which is illustrated on page vii in the Appendix.

Letter 1

Dictator: T. L. Powers, Administrative Assistant

Addressee: Mr. Jack Robertson, Director, Maritime Commission, 1511 Alaskan Way, Seattle, WA 98101

Background: Mr. Powers is notifying Mr. Robertson about a traffic problem which may occur in the bay on the following Thursday. (Compose an appropriate subject line.)

20-C. Executive Language in Manufacturing

claimant (klām′ ənt), n. person who makes a claim.

concealed (kən sēl′ d), v. 1. to keep secret or prevent disclosure. 2. hide or place out of sight.

discrepancies (dis krep′ ən sēz), n. 1. inconsistent. 2. difference or disagreement.

20-D. Communication in Manufacturing

BACKGROUND FOR COMMUNICATION #1. Improper handling of merchandise or equipment received by departments when shortages, damaged or defective merchandise has been delivered has led the Office of the Contracting and Purchasing Officer to send a memo to all department managers regarding procedures to be followed.

Lesson 20

Page 65

Letter 2
(Office-Style Dictation)

Dictator: Mr. N. L. Patton, Service Manager

Addressee: Miss Barbara Christensen, 1914 Hudson Street, Bloomington, IN 47401

Background: Mr. Patton is describing what an investigation of the addressee's car has revealed.

BACKGROUND FOR COMMUNICATION #2. This memo directs the department managers regarding the proper procedure for returning merchandise or equipment and for canceled purchase orders.

canceled, permission, replacement, clearly, instructions, approved, cancellations

BACKGROUND FOR COMMUNICATION #3. In this memo to the department managers the Office of the Contracting and Purchasing Officer outlines the procedure for sending equipment to a factory or service center for repairs.

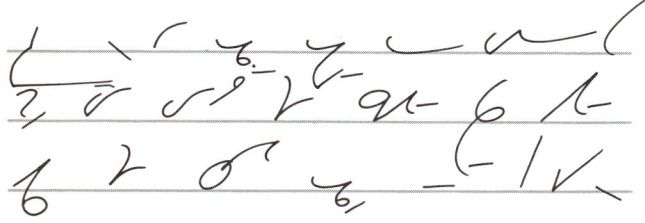

LESSON 21

21-A. System Control

Phrases beginning with *as you* are stressed in the notes below.

21-B. THE OFFICE: A Decision-Making Center

UNIT 4 COMMUNICATION IN PSYCHOLOGY

52-C. Executive Language in Transportation

rapid transit (rap′id tran′sit), n. a form of local public transportation usually transporting passengers between suburban points and the city.

right-of-way (rīt ov wā), n. strip of land on which railroad tracks are laid, highways are constructed, or power lines are built.

ad valorem (ad və lô′rəm), adj. Latin term meaning in proportion to the value.

52-D. Communication in Transportation

Letter 1

Dictator: Mr. Guy Stover, County Commissioner

Addressee: Mayor R. A. Adams, Biloxi City Hall, Biloxi, MS 39530

Background: Mr. Stover, chairman of the County Commissioners, is sending a progress report to the Mayor on the rapid transit railway system, which is to be constructed.

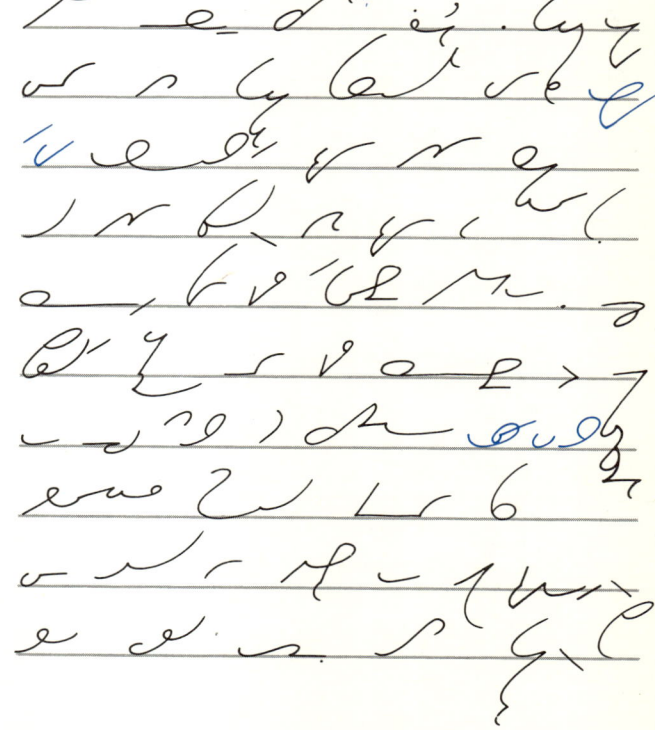

21-C. Professional Language in Psychology

accredited (ə kred′ ə tid), adj. 1. belief, approval; worthy of acceptance. 2. recognized as maintaining a high quality of standards.

auspice (ôs′ pis), n. 1. patronage and guidance. 2. a prophetic sign or omen. 3. favorable circumstance or indication of success.

grandfather clause, n. a clause which creates an exemption based on previously existing circumstances.

prerequisite (pre rek′ wə zit), n. something necessary to obtain an end or carry out a function.

Lesson 52

21-D. Communication in Psychology

BACKGROUND FOR COMMUNICATION #1. The state Legislature has passed an act regarding the certifying and licensing of psychologists. This memo is written in response to inquiries about the status of psychologists already practicing in the state and the effect of the "grandfather clause."

BACKGROUND FOR COMMUNICATION #2. Because of the many inquiries received concerning certification by specialty, the Board has decided to send out a memo explaining its point of view on the question and also about the supervision of psychological associates.

specialty, ethics, adopted, specifically, adequately, prohibited, independent, professional, actions

BACKGROUND FOR COMMUNICATION #3. The State Board of Examiners of Psychologists decided to send a memo to psychologists in the state about some of the board's activities and to call their attention to a recent article the Board feels worthy of mention. The memo is dictated in office style.

Lesson 21

LESSON 52

52-A. System Control

This exercise, which deals with the cost of operating a car, contains 140 standard words. Your instructor will preview the article and then dictate it until you can record it easily in one minute.

52-B. THE OFFICE: A Decision-Making Center

Lesson 52

Page 161

LESSON 22

22-A. Effective Display Guidelines

STATIONERY DESIGN FOR INTERNAL COMMUNICATIONS. In designing stationery for internal communications, the office manager will be most concerned with selecting a format that will effect speed (a) in recording the message to be sent, (b) in distributing the message, and (c) in the reading of the message by the recipient.

To achieve this conservation of time, the office manager will usually adopt a standard form for recording such information as the name of the addressee, the originator of the memo, the date of the memo, and the subject. Use of printed "direction signals," such as "To," "From," "Date," and "Subject" speeds the transcription of the message, its distribution, and its reading by the recipient.

The number of printed elements varies, depending on the type of business. An insurance firm, for example, may need the element "Policy No." Another firm might need "Address" for branch offices. Regardless of the type of business, however, at least four items should be included: "To," "From," "Date," and "Subject."

Arrangement of the "direction signals" should be such that tabulating for various positions is minimized. Note in the first memo heading below that all of the items can be filled in using only one tab stop.

To further speed typing, the printed elements should be spaced so that the variable line spacer does not have to be used to line up the typed copy with printed elements.

Executive Offices — STANDARD PUMPS, INCORPORATED — *Interoffice Correspondence*
476 Pacific Avenue • Portland, Oregon 97210 • 361-6311

To:
From:
Date:
Subject:

Stimson Products Corporation — INTEROFFICE CORRESPONDENCE
490 MAIN BOULEVARD • DENVER, COLORADO 80202 • 623-6107

To: From: Date:
Subject: Policy No.:

Davis Equipment Company

INTEROFFICE COMMUNICATION

TO: SUBJECT:
FROM: DATE:

Printed Headings on Memorandum Stationery

51-D. Proofreading Exercise

The following letter contains 25 errors in grammar, spelling, punctuation, word division, word choice, letter style, or typewriting. Type a copy of the material as it appears in this exercise; then edit your typed copy, making the necessary corrections in pen or pencil. Begin the date on line 12 and use a 1-inch left margin.

Febuary 5, 19--

Ruth Mason
Kappa Delta House
1519 Campus Drive
Boise, ID. 83706

Dear Miss Mason

How would you like to combine a semester of college work with a trip around the world? You can do just that when you enroll in the World University Afloat program.

Yes, now there is a way for you to become acquainted with fascinating points all over the world. Whats more, you may earn college credit for this educational experience. The Parthenon may become a class room for a lecture on ancient Greece. A ride on a sampan in Hong Kong may provide a sociological view of it's floating society. You may study Gothic architecture in the shadows of Westminster Abbey. You may analyze a great opera after hearing a magnificent performance at La Scala. These are but a few of the famous places that you will visit as you tour the world.

The World University Afloat enrolls two groups of 500 students every year. There campus is the S.S. Birmingham. This vessell is equipped with modern educational facilities including a well stocked library. Students follow a comprehensive curiculum under the direction of a highly-qualified faculty. It is possible for them to earn a semester of accredited college work as they experience one of the most enchanting adventures of their lifes.

World University Afloat is now excepting enrollments for the spring and fall semesters of next year. The spring semester tour circles the world from Los Angeles, stops in Asia and Africa, and ends in New York. The fall semester tour depart from New York and has port stops in Europe, Africa, and Latin American. The tour ends in Los Angeles.

Send now for the World University Afloat catalog which contains detailed information about this novel educational opportunity. A seperate brochure will give you information about costs and financial aid programs. An order form and addressed envelop is enclosed for your convience.

Yours truely

Robert James
Registrar

rj np

Lesson 51   Page 160

22-B. Transcription Craftsmanship

REINSERTION FOR CORRECTION. Occasionally, an error is not detected until the typescript has been removed from the machine. If the mistake is correctable, the secretary should make the correction rather than retype the page. There are two reasons for not retyping the page. First, stationery would be wasted, which raises office costs. Second, there is no certainty that additional errors will not be made, thus consuming even more time than calculated for errorless retyping.

To minimize the cost of lost time for corrections, the following practices should be observed:

1. Erase the error immediately on all copies. The sooner the error is removed the less time the ink has to soak into the paper, thus making removal easier. Protect the adjacent typing with 5 x 3 cards or by using an eraser shield.

2. Correct the file copy first. By "practicing" on the file copy, you will be more likely to make an undetectable correction on the original.

To be certain of good vertical lineup, slip a sheet of scratch paper into the machine, type a few words, noting the distance between the bottom of the letters and the alignment scale.

In inserting the file copy, use a backing sheet behind it, especially if lightweight manifold paper is used for file copies.

Horizontal alignment can be made most easily by aligning the typed line according to letters like "i" or "t."

When the copy is thought to be aligned, the ribbon lever can be switched to "Stencil" and the correct letter struck. The faint impression will reveal whether further adjustment of the paper is necessary.

A carbon impression can be made on the file copy rather easily, and making one will cause the correction to be less detectable than would be a ribbon impression. Just cut a 2-inch square of carbon paper and one of bond paper. Staple the bond paper square to the back (uncoated) side of the carbon paper square.

Line up the typescript at the point at which the correct letter is to be inserted. Place the stapled squares between the ribbon and the file copy with the carbon paper surface next to the file copy. Strike the correct letter, and a carbon impression will be made.

If several carbon copies have been made, as each carbon copy is aligned for correction, additional squares of bond paper can be attached behind the carbon paper square, thus enabling the correction to be a "match" for surrounding copy.

3. If a manual typewriter is used, the correction on the original can be "matched" with the surrounding copy by striking the letter key lightly as many times as necessary for the desired darkness of impression.

If an electric typewriter is used, the touch control can be changed to effect a "matched" impression.

If by chance the impression is too dark, the letter can be touched lightly with plastic cleaner to lighten the impression.

Making a Carbon Impression on Reinserted Copy

Words

Letter 2

Dictator: R. P. Steinbaugh, Director

Addressee: Taylor Shipping Company, 5196 Battery Avenue, Charleston, SC 29407

Background: Mr. Steinbaugh is informing the Taylor Shipping Company of recent changes in shipping regulations. He would like this letter brought to the attention of A. S. Thorne, Shipping Manager.

certified, lubrication, ammunition, caterpillar, axle, textile, tariff, licensees, consignees, transit, commissioner

Letter 3
(to be dictated)

Dictator: Frances Sadoff, Executive Secretary, Clayton Airport Board

Addressees: Mr. J. T. Bradley, 2104 Lakeview Drive, Billings, MT 59101

Background: Miss Sadoff is sending Mr. Bradley a preliminary report on airport operations. Send a carbon copy of this letter to Harry Spencer, Manager, Clayton Airport, Billings, MT 59101

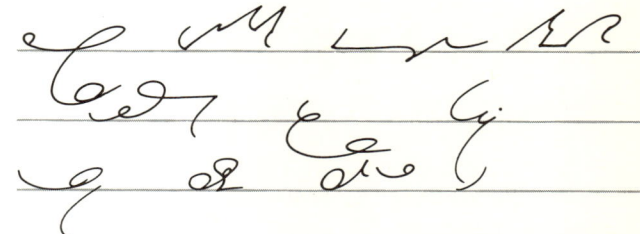

elaborate, statistics, commuter, discontinues, revamp, seaplane, prohibitive, liability, aviation, advisory

Lesson 51   Page 159

22-C. Communication in Psychology

BACKGROUND FOR COMMUNICATION #5. The State Board of Examiners of Psychologists issues a bulletin in answer to many queries received about its activities since its creation by the Legislature and appointment by the Governor.

DIRECTIONS TO THE TRANSCRIBER. This bulletin is to be typed in single-spaced paragraph form with a 70-space line. The heading is to be typed as for previous bulletins, i.e., in solid caps. One file copy is to be made.

22-D. Transcription Capsules

The following paragraphs are excerpts from communications pertinent to the psychological profession. Use a 70-space line and single space the paragraphs.

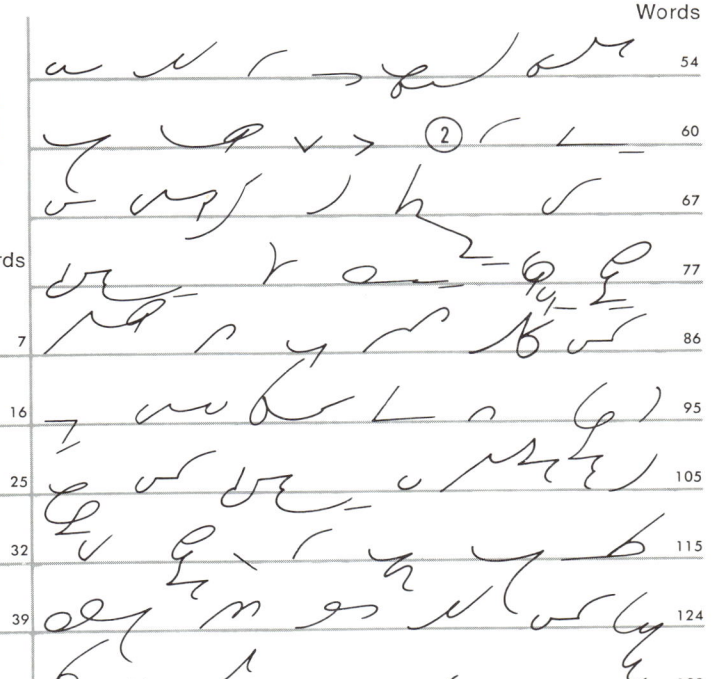

LESSON 23

23-A. System Control

Automatization of phrases beginning with *you will* is stressed in the shorthand notes below.

23-B. THE OFFICE: A Decision-Making Center

LESSON 51

51-A. Signals in Written Communication

ATTENTION LINE. An attention line is used when an individual addresses a business letter to a firm but wishes to make sure that a certain individual within that firm sees the message. Since the letter has been addressed to the firm, it could be opened by someone other than the individual named in the attention line or his secretary should they both happen to be away from the office for a period of several days. Therefore, if the message required immediate attention, action could be initiated at once by another person within the firm.

51-B. Transcription Craftsmanship

TIPS ON TYPING ATTENTION LINES. In a business letter the attention line is typed a double space below the inside address. It is usually typed even with the left margin; although it is sometimes centered. The salutation is typed a double space below the attention line. Since the letter is addressed to a firm, the appropriate salutation is *Gentlemen*. Three commonly used attention-line styles appear below.

```
The Alton Manufacturing Company
Box 312
Alton, IL  62002

Attention Mr. Keith Brandon
Gentlemen:
```

```
The Alton Manufacturing Company
Box 312
Alton, IL  62002

Attention:  Mr. Keith Brandon
Gentlemen:
```

```
The Alton Manufacturing Company
Box 312
Alton, IL  62002

ATTENTION:  Mr. Keith Brandon
Gentlemen:
```

The U. S. Postal Service recommends that the attention line on the envelope be placed on the line below the firm name in the address block.

```
The Alton Manufacturing Company
Attention Mr. Keith Brandon
Box 312
Alton, IL  62002
```

51-C. Transcription Letters

Use block style and open punctuation for the letters in this lesson.

Letter 1

Dictator: Thomas Bartuska, General Manager, Tri-Cities Airport

Addressee: Tri-Cities Aviation Commission, County Courthouse, Richland, WA 99352

Background: In this letter to the Tri-Cities Aviation Commission, Mr. Bartuska wants to bring the members up to date on the most recent plans for the new airport terminal. He would like to have this letter called to the attention of Mr. George L. Scott, Chairman of the Commission. He would also like to have a carbon copy sent to Keen and Sloan, Architects, 1500 Aspen Street, Portland, OR 97222.

UNIT 10 COMMUNICATION IN TRANSPORTATION

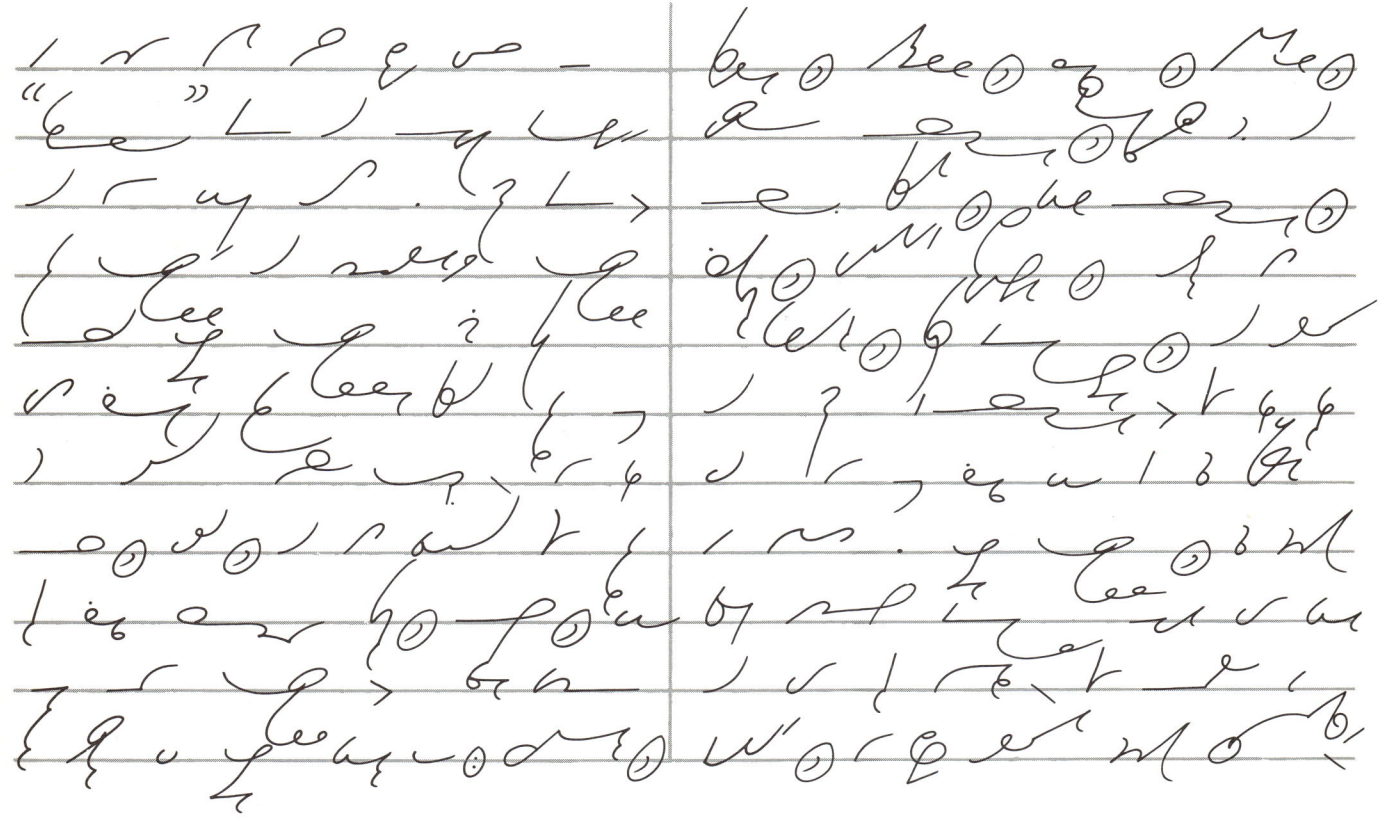

Accountant's Handbook
Bartlett's Familiar Quotations
Black's Law Dictionary
The Congressional Directory
Foreign Commerce and Navigation of the United States
Guide to American Directories
Hotel Red Book
The Legal Secretary's Complete Handbook
The Monthly Catalog of U.S. Government Publications
National Associations of the United States
Patterson's American Educational Directory
Polk's Bank Directory
Rand McNally-Standard World Atlas
Reader's Guide to Periodical Literature
Roget's Thesaurus
The Statistical Abstract of the United States
Thomas' Register of American Manufacturers
Webster's Third New International Dictionary
The World Almanac
The Monthly Labor Review

A Partial List of Sources of Information

50-D. Proofreading Exercise

The letter on this page contains 35 errors in grammar, spelling, punctuation, word division, word choice, letter style, or typewriting. Type a copy of the material as it appears in this exercise; then edit your copy, making the necessary corrections in pen or pencil. Begin on line 12 and set a one-inch left margin.

Febuary 17, 19--

Allen Rupp Jr.
519 Gomber St.
Cambridge, OH

Dear Mr. Ropp:

It is a pleasure, Mr. Rupp, to send you information concerning the job of an hospital administrator. I have served in this capacity for 7 years. It is a demanding and a challanging job, but it is also a rewarding one.

My job at Community Hospital is simply put to run the institution. I report direct to the Community Hospital Board of Trusties. I must see that our hospital is properly staffed, that it has adequate facilities, that it operates efficiently, that it meets acreditation standards, that it follows governmental regulations, that it operates with in budgeted revenues. I must coordinate the work of about 20 professional groups and about two dozen Departments.

Many fine schools now offer a two year graduate program in hospital administration. Some graduate schools prefer liberal arts graduates, others prefer students with degrees in Business Administration. Of course, you must have a B.A. or a B.S. and a respectible academic record.

Beginning assistant administrators with a Master's degree earn from $7,500 to $15,000 depending upon their responsibilities and the size of the hospital. Administrator salaries range from $12,000 to $35,000.

Some administrators are working in the area of preventive hospitalization, that is, they administer programs that will keep people out of hospitals. They develop area health centers, nursing homes, and out-patient clinics. Such facilities have become increasing important as the cost of health care has raised and as hospital facilities can no longer meet the needs of their clientel.

Most hospital administrators are affilliated with the American College of Hospital Administrators. I am enclosing a brochure on hospital administration which it publishes.

Yours Truly,

Carlton Scott
Hospital Administrator

cs sm

23-C. Professional Language in Psychology

electroencephalogram (en sef′ ə lə gram), n. tracing of brain waves made by an electroencephalograf.

IQ or **I.Q.**, intelligence quotient.

perceptual (pər sep′ chủ əl), adj. of or having to do with perception.

23-D. Communication in Psychology

BACKGROUND FOR COMMUNICATION #1. A psychologist reports to Dr. Kramer, a pediatrician concerning the results of his observations and testing of a child patient, Helen Briggs.

Letter 2

Dictator: J. L. Parker, Executive Secretary of the Browne County Medical Association.

Addressee: Dr. George A. Mills, 219 Federal Building, Wilmington, DE 19801

Background: Mr. Parker is notifying Browne County Medical Association members about the December meeting and their dues for the following year. He wishes to have a form typed at the bottom of the letter, which can then be returned by the addressee.

Letter 3
(to be dictated)

Dictator: Paul C. Cranston, Chairman, Drug Forum Committee

Addressee: Dr. Clarence Knapp, Box 2310, Green Forest, AR 72638

Background: Mr. Cranston is inviting Dr. Knapp to speak at a forthcoming drug forum which is to be held at Forest Springs Community College. He wishes to have a carbon copy of the letter sent to Jim Dunn, Student Senate President.

Forest, forum, depth, adolescents, eminently, auditorium, videotape, television

Lesson 50 — Page 155

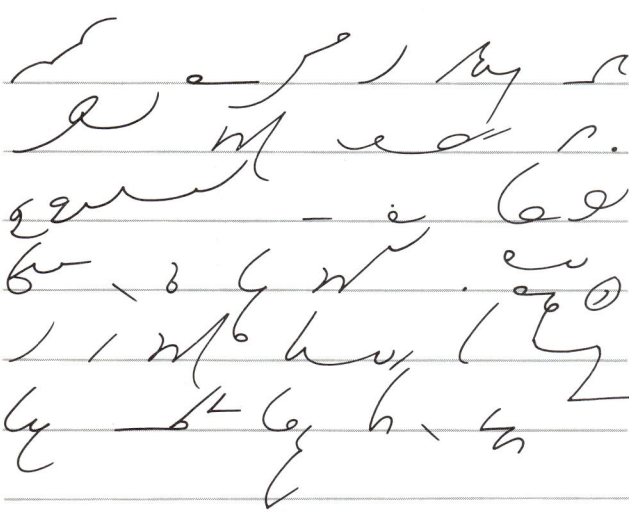

BACKGROUND FOR COMMUNICATION #2. A psychological consulting firm that markets tests for psychologists announces the publication of two new ones.

thoroughly, proven, valid, intelligence, administer, verbal, production, technical, descriptions

BACKGROUND FOR COMMUNICATION #3. The psychologist who had written to Dr. Kramer about Helen Briggs writes a follow-up letter to report evidence of improvement in the behavior of the patient. The communication will be dictated in office style.

LESSON 24

24-A. Effective Display Guidelines

STATIONERY DESIGN FOR EXTERNAL COMMUNICATIONS. In designing stationery for external communications, the office manager will be most concerned with the effectiveness of the stationery as a symbol of his firm. Does the paper used and the design of the letterhead leave an appropriate and favorable impression on the recipient of the letter? Does it "sell" the receiver of the message on the company because of its quality and attractiveness?

The letterhead designs on business stationery differ greatly in depth, ranging from less than 1 inch to 3¾ inches. The designs may be "balanced" or "unbalanced." The design must be taken into consideration by the transcriber in selecting the letter style that looks most attractive for the message to be transcribed.

Among the letterhead factors of concern are the adequacy of information given on the letterhead; i.e., address and telephone information or "reply to" information such as person, department, or division. He is concerned with paper costs for certain weights and qualities, printing costs (including color), and cost of various sizes of stationery that might be needed.

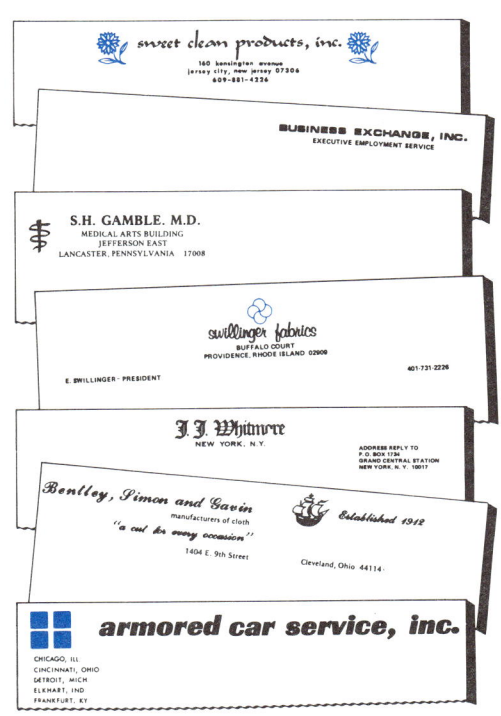

Letterhead Designs of Various Depths

50-C. Transcription Letters

INSTRUCTIONS FOR TRANSCRIPTION LETTERS 1, 2, AND 3: Use modified block style and open punctuation. See page v of the Appendix.

Letter 1

Dictator: J. Paul Penney, M. D.

Addressee: Mr. Gordon B. Blake, Personnel Director, National Silicon Chemicals, Deer River, MN 56636

Background: Dr. Penney is sending a treatment report on an employee to the NSC Personnel Director. He would like a carbon copy sent to the University Medicenter Records Department.

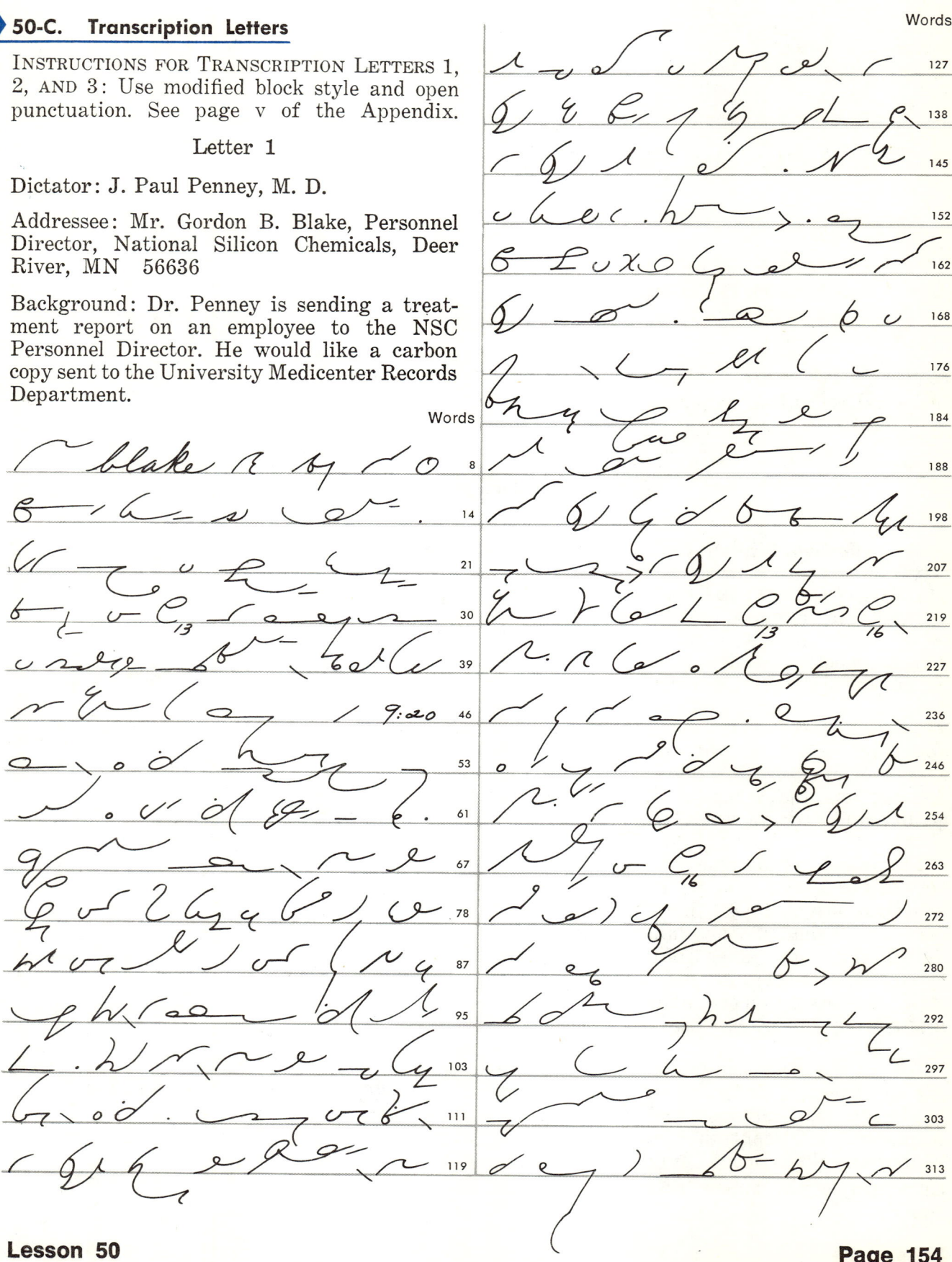

Some firms have guide marks printed on their stationery to indicate the placement of various parts of the letter or where the letter is to be folded. Sometimes these guide marks are large enough to be plainly visible after the letter has been typed; others are small and so lightly printed that after the letter has been typed, they cannot be seen. Some marks are dots; some, straight lines; some brackets.

A firm may have printed stationery for second and succeeding pages of multipage letters. Usually the printed matter for this purpose is limited to the company name in small type but matching that on the letterhead.

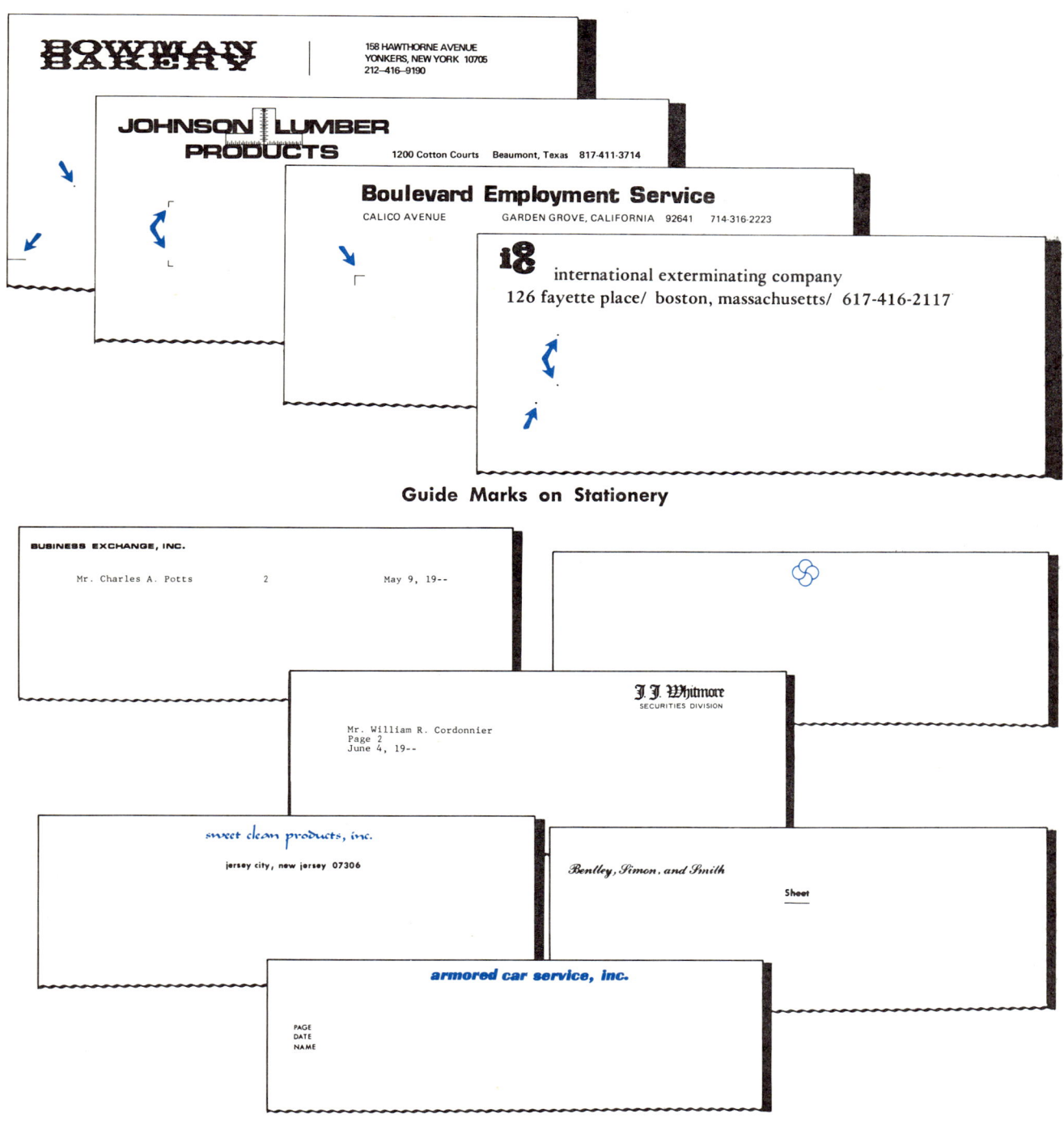

Guide Marks on Stationery

Printed Continuation Sheets

LESSON 50

50-A. Signals in Written Communications

COMBINATION LETTER-FORM. In order to save time and expense, an individual who requests routine information may use a combination letter-form similar to the one that is illustrated below. The use of this device also saves time, energy, and expense for the addressee. He need not compose and prepare a reply letter.

```
    Thursday, May 12, at 1:30 p.m.  Please indicate on the form below
    whether you plan to attend the luncheon and/or the afternoon session.
                            Sincerely


                            (Miss) Nancy Post, Chairman
- - - - - - - - - - - - - - - - - - - - - - - - - - - - - - - - - - - -
            (Use hyphen key for perforation mark.)

    ____ Yes, I plan to attend the luncheon on May 12.

    ____ I will be unable to attend the luncheon on May 12, but
         I hope to attend the afternoon session.

                            _____
                                       Name
```

50-B. Transcription Craftsmanship

TIPS ON PREPARING MULTICOPIES. When she prepares multiple copies, the secretary may have at her disposal a number of media, which she may use. They include: carbon copies, spirit masters, stencils, offset mats, carbon sets, no carbon required sets, input media for automatic typewriters, or photocopies. The secretary must use good judgment as she determines the most suitable means to use in terms of appearance, use, cost, and time.

Secretaries who prepare multicopies with conventional carbon paper should observe the following points: (1) Select a carbon paper weight that is appropriate for the number of copies you are preparing, the type style you use, the kind of typewriter you use, and the kind of stationery you use. (2) Assemble carbon packs in an efficient manner to avoid excessive handling and wasted time. (3) Cut the corners from your carbon paper so that you can disassemble a carbon pack quickly by holding the carbon pack in the upper left corner while pulling the protruding carbon sheets from the bottom edge of the pack. (4) After inserting the carbon pack in your typewriter, release and then re-engage the paper release lever to avoid wrinkles and trees on your carbon copies. (5) Be sure to adjust the carbon copy gauges on your typewriter to correspond with the number of carbon copies you are planning to make. (6) Rotate your carbon paper end for end as you reuse it for even wear.

24-B. Transcription Craftsmanship

COMMERCIAL COVER-UP PRODUCTS FOR CORRECTIONS. Being marketed as alternatives to the traditional erasers are "cover-up" products. These products are principally of two kinds: coated paper and a white liquid sometimes called *correction fluid*.

The coated paper is manufactured in sheets of perforated strips or in "Scotch-tape" dispenser form. At least one brand of coated paper has a slightly different coating for strips to be used in correcting originals from that used for correcting carbon copies.

The procedure for using the coated paper is as follows:

1. Move the carriage back to the point of the error. Place a square or strip of the coated paper between the ribbon and the original. If carbon copies are being made, a square or strip must be placed between each carbon paper surface and the copy it faces.

2. To cover up the error, strike the same letter that was struck in making the mistake.

3. Remove the square or squares.

4. Backspace again to the covered-up letter and strike the correct letter.

The advantages of this type of product are that (1) it may be faster for the transcriber who is not proficient with traditional erasing, and (2) there is no problem of erasing without smudging or smearing adjacent copy.

The disadvantages are: (1) the coating wears off in time; (2) the "cover-up" may not be complete if a new fabric ribbon or a one-time ribbon is being used; (3) if a carbon copy is being corrected, the coating comes off on the face of the carbon paper so that the next time that carbon sheet is used a letter struck at that point will not print or will print imperfectly; and (4) the corrections on the carbon copies will not be good.

The liquid product comes in a bottle with a brush applicator attached to the cap. Some manufacturers include a bottle of thinner to be used if the fluid becomes too thick for proper application.

The correction fluid type of cover-up material is used as follows:

1. Turn the papers in the machine up a few lines. Cover the error with a light stroke of the brush, being careful not to put too much on.

2. Line up the transcript to the point of the covered-up error, after the fluid has dried. If errors are corrected on carbon copies, hold the copies apart until the drying process is complete.

The correction fluid has the same advantages as the coated paper. It also has the advantage of being permanent; i.e., it won't rub off. This product is good for covering up errors on material to be photographed; it is also good for rough drafts. The more opaque the material the less detectable the correction.

The disadvantages are: (1) the liquid must be dry before corrections can be made; (2) the cover-up is quite noticeable on lightweight or colored paper, which is used frequently for carbon copies; (3) the fluid may come off onto the face of the carbon paper, as it does with the coated paper.

The effectiveness of the cover-up products depends upon the surface on which it is used (its opacity, weight, etc.), whether carbon copies are to be corrected, and the skill of the corrector.

One important disadvantage of the cover-up products is that connected with the making of copies of the transcript. If certain heat-process copying machines are used, covered-up errors appear on the copies as strikeovers. Those firms receiving such copies may have the impression that the original was sent out with strikeovers on it, thus leaving a bad impression of the sending firm.

49-C. Professional Language in Medicine

caries (kăr′ ēz), n. decay of the teeth.

dental calculus (den′ tl kal′ kyə ləs), n. tartar that accumulates on teeth.

dental hygienist (den′ tl hī′ jēn ist), n. person trained to clean teeth and assist a dentist in his work.

49-D. Communication in Medicine

Letter 1

Dictator: Dr. Donald Riedel

Addressee: Mr. William P. Burns, 2404 Kenny Drive, Pullman, WA 99163

Background: Dr. Riedel is reminding Mr. Burns of his dental examination appointment and giving him some information on preventive dentistry.

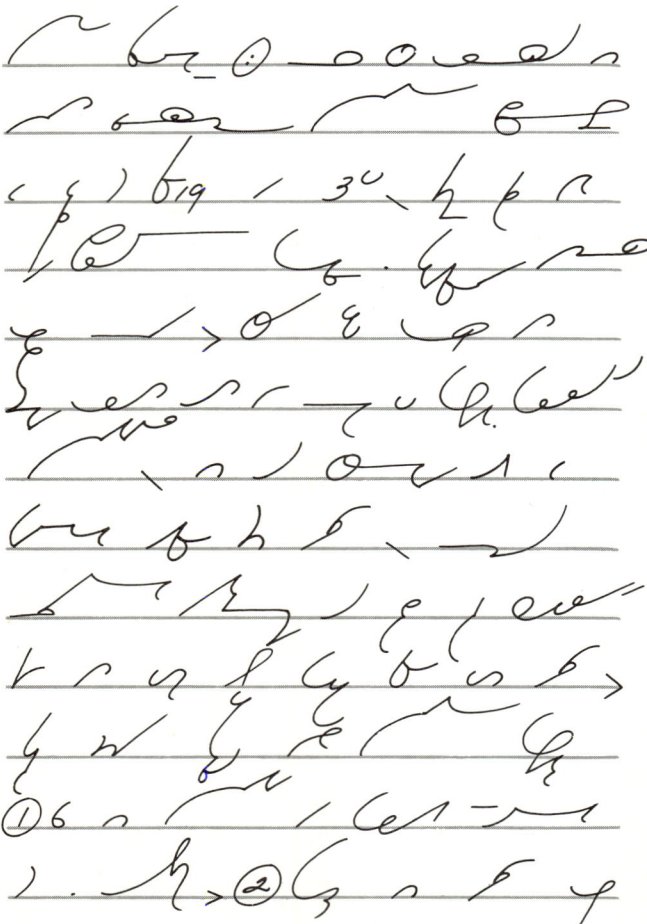

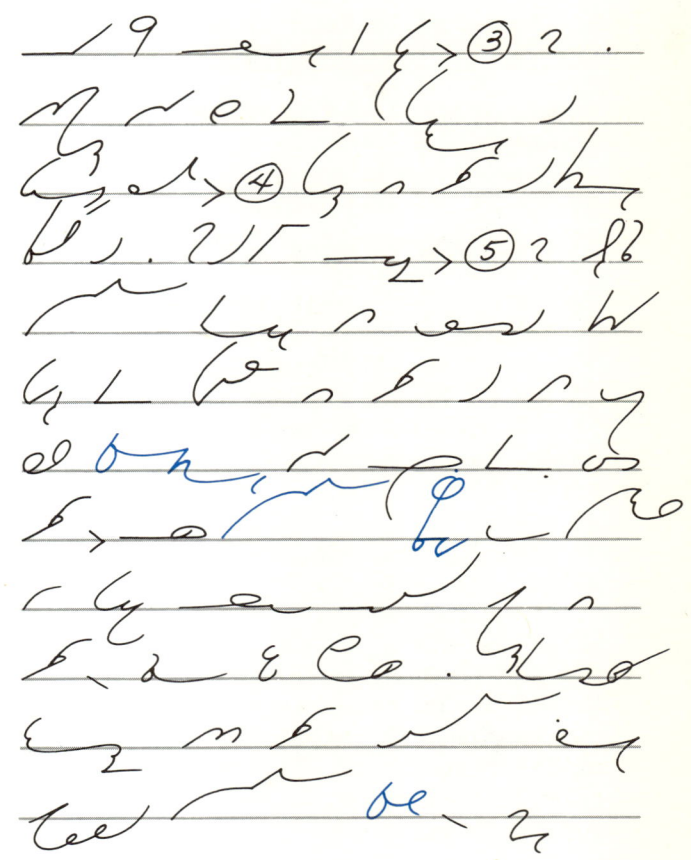

Letter 2
(Office-Style Dictation)

Dictator: Dr. C. C. Calhoun

Addressee: Mrs. Richard Hicks, 2098 South Braden Avenue, Tulsa, OK 74112

Background: Dr. Calhoun, a pediatrician, is giving professional advice to Mrs. Hicks concerning her baby's formula and sleeping arrangements.

formula, feedings, ounces, liquid, refrigerated, sanitary, sterilize, children's, mattresses, blankets, temperature, sickness, nurse

24-C. Communication in Psychology

BACKGROUND FOR THE COMMUNICATION. The State Board of Examiners of Psychologists has been asked to clarify who is properly identified as a "psychologist" under the law.

DIRECTIONS TO THE TRANSCRIBER. The centered heading should be typed in solid caps. A 70-space line should be used, and the quoted matter should be indented five spaces from both margins. A file copy should be made.

[Shorthand notes]

24-D. Transcription Capsules

[Shorthand notes]

Lesson 49

LESSON 25

25-A. System Control

Phrases beginning with *we should* are illustrated below.

25-B. THE OFFICE: A Decision-Making Center

LESSON 49

49-A. System Control

[Shorthand content]

49-B. THE OFFICE: A Decision-Making Center

[Shorthand content] (see 47-B)

▶ **25-C. Professional Language in Psychology**

auditory (ô′ də tô′ rē), adj. of or related to hearing; sense of hearing; organs of hearing.

distractible (dis trak′ tə bəl), adj. that which can be distracted.

medication (med′ ə kā′ shən), n. process of treating with medicine.

▶ **25-D. Communication in Psychology**

BACKGROUND FOR COMMUNICATION #1. A psychologist reports his findings to Dr. Kramer, a pediatrician, after seeing and testing Mike Jones, a child brought to him by his mother.

Lesson 25   Page 80

48-D. Proofreading Exercise

The letter on this page contains 35 errors in grammar, spelling, punctuation, word division, word choice, letter style, or typewriting. Type a copy of the material as it appears in this exercise; then edit your copy, making the necessary corrections in pen or pencil. Begin on line 12 and set a one-inch left margin.

February 28, 19--

Office Employment Service
1208 West Beach Boulevard
Biloxi, Miss. 39530

Gentlemen:

I need your aide in securing a nurse receptionist. Eileen Trent who has worked with me for the past four years plans to resign.

Miss Trent makes appointments, recieves callers, and screens telephone calls. She serves as a liaison between hospital personel and I. She takes care of my correspondance, bookeeping, and medical records. She serves as my medical libarian. In addition, she releives my attending nurse when necessary.

Because of the nature of the job it is necessary for me to employ a versitale person who is reliable and industrous. She must be well-groomed and posess a pleasing personality. She must be able to implement sound office procedures. She must also be an excellent stenographer. While it would be good, if she were to have some nursing practice, it is not absolutely necessary, however, she must be willing to learn nursing skills on the job.

My office hours are from 9:30 a.m. to 5:30 p.m. Monday through Friday. Because my work load each day is somewhat unpredictable, my employees must be willing to work over-time when I run behind schedule. Each of my employees have a one hour lunch period. Both my nurse and my receptionist is expected to wear neat uniforms.

Starting pay for this position is $175 per week. Fringe benefits include free health and hospitalisation insurance. Each employee receives a two-week vacation during their first five years' of employment and three-weeks after that period. My suite is attractive, spacious, and air conditioned. The facilities are up-to-date.

Would you please have potential candidates phone Miss Trent at MA2-1198.

Sincerely,

John Parlette, M.D.

JP/ET

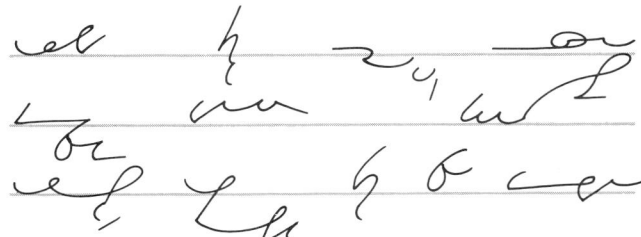

BACKGROUND FOR COMMUNICATION #2. The psychologist reports to Dr. Kramer on the results of a retest on Mike Jones.

retest, fusses, neurological, minor, comparison, strong, coordination, relaxed, reflects, pushes, par, semester

BACKGROUND FOR COMMUNICATION #3. This communication concerns the report of a follow-up visit by Mike, three months after the second visit.

alerted, increasingly, regression, thoughtless, contained, essentially, typical, potential, inability, immaturity, achievement, obvious, injured

BACKGROUND FOR COMMUNICATION #4. In this fourth communication regarding Mike, the psychologist reports to Dr. Kramer regarding some improvement in Mike's performance generally and in the school situation. The communication will be dictated in office style.

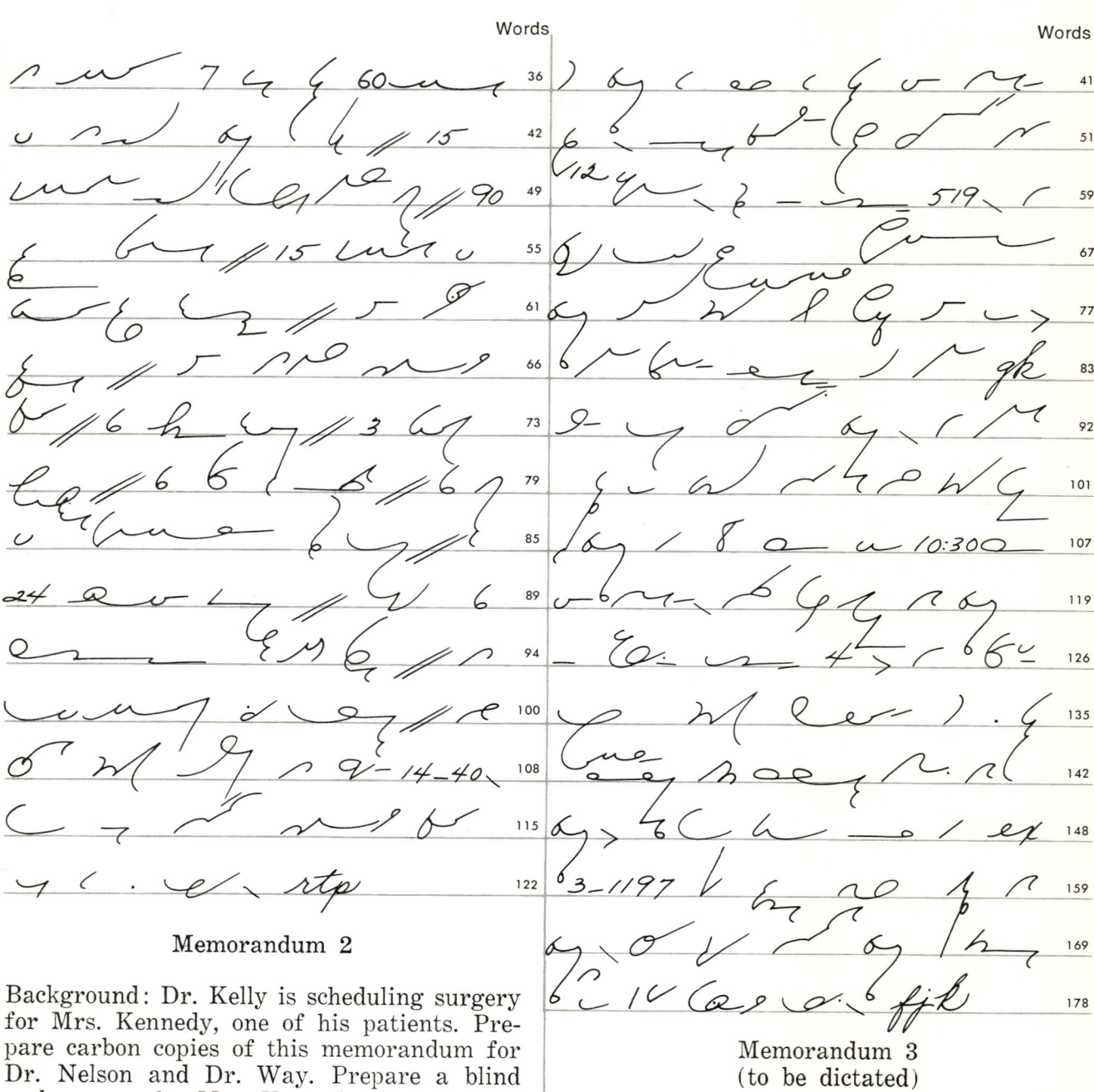

Memorandum 2

Background: Dr. Kelly is scheduling surgery for Mrs. Kennedy, one of his patients. Prepare carbon copies of this memorandum for Dr. Nelson and Dr. Way. Prepare a blind carbon copy for Mrs. Kennedy.

Memorandum 3
(to be dictated)

Dictator: Jack L. Garden, Hospital Administrator

Addressee: All Southeastern City Hospital Personnel

Background: In this memorandum, Mr. Garden is notifying hospital personnel of a preliminary planning meeting for the proposed Southeastern Medicenter. Prepare a carbon copy for M. S. Landers, chief architect for the project.

LESSON 26

26-A. System Control

In the System Control exercises for Lessons 26 through 35, you will be attempting to automatize notetaking of dictation consisting largely of words included in the 1,500 most-used words in business correspondence.

If you can write a sentence twice from dictation in 15 seconds, you will be notetaking at 80 wam; in 12 seconds, at 100 wam; in 10 seconds, at 120 wam; in 8½ seconds, approximately at 140 wam; in 7½ seconds, at 160 wam; in 6 seconds, at 200 wam.

26-B. THE OFFICE: A Decision-Making Center

LESSON 48

48-A. Signals in Written Communications

CARBON-COPY NOTATIONS. Carbon-copy notations are placed on business correspondence for two reasons: (1) to notify the addressee which individuals were sent copies of the letter or memorandum, and (2) to record on the sender's file copy the names of those individuals to whom copies of the correspondence were sent.

When the sender does not wish the addressee to know that a copy of his letter or memorandum has been sent to someone else, a blind carbon-copy notation is used. This notation, which does not appear on the addressee's letter, still provides a record of the recipients of the carbon copies on the sender's file copy.

48-B. Transcription Craftsmanship

TIPS ON TYPING CARBON-COPY NOTATIONS. A carbon-copy notation is usually placed on the original and all carbon copies of the correspondence. It is typed at the left margin a double space below the reference initials or the enclosure notation, whichever appears last. One of the following styles may be used:

```
cc Mr. Jones        cc: Grand Trucking Company        CC: Mr. T. L. Poppin
                                                          Mrs. H. J. Benson
```

The blind carbon-copy notation is placed at the left margin two or three lines from the top edge of the appropriate carbon copies. One of the following styles may be used:

```
bcc Mr. Jones       bcc: Grand Trucking Company       BCC: Mr. T. L. Poppin
                                                           Mrs. H. J. Benson
```

On an informal memorandum sent to more than one person in the office, the secretary sometimes prepares extra carbon copies of the correspondence rather than having to type an original copy for each recipient.

In such instances, the following style may be used in the "TO:" section of the memorandum heading. Notice a check mark is placed after the name of the individual to whom the respective copy is to go.

```
TO:  Mr. James Smith
     Mr. Homer Dana
     Miss Barbara Christensen ✓
```

48-C. Transcription Items

Use Memorandum Style #2 illustrated on page i in the Appendix for the following transcription items.

Memorandum 1

Background: Ruth T. Page is the floor supervisor for Ward 7. This memorandum is an order for hospital supplies for her ward. Send a carbon copy to Alma James, who is assistant supervisor for Ward 7.

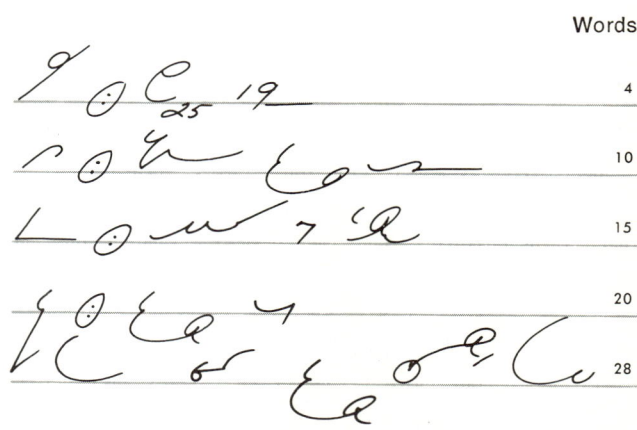

Words: 4, 10, 15, 20, 28

26-C. Executive Language in Printing and Publishing

plating (plāt′ ing), n. 1. the act or art of covering a surface with a plate or coating of metal. 2. the forming of metal into plates; making a plate from type for printing.

prospectus (prə spek′ təs), n. a printed statement used to describe a business to prospective buyers, investors, etc.

typesetting (tip′ set′ ing), n. the process of setting type for printing; adj. used for setting type.

26-D. Communication in Printing and Publishing

BACKGROUND FOR COMMUNICATION #1. This memo welcomes new staff to the Editorial Department of the Crown Educational Book Company and explains the philosophy of the firm.

Addressee: Mrs. Laura Clarke, 1212 Cook Drive, Sioux City, IA 51103

Background: Mrs. Clarke recently went to Dr. Pelton for her annual physical examination. Now that the laboratory tests have been completed, Dr. Pelton is reporting the findings to her.

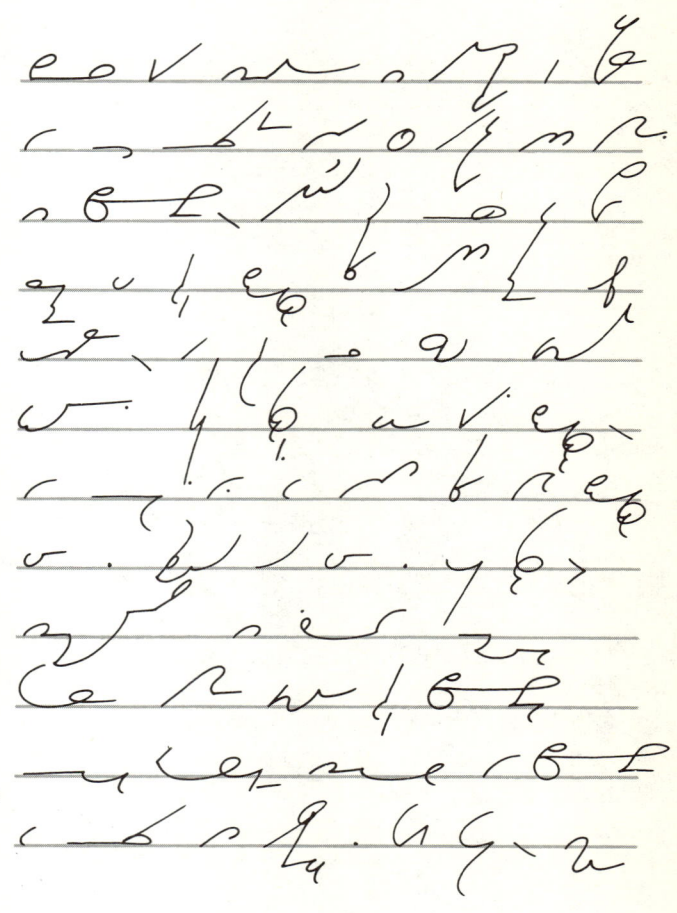

Letter 2
(Office-Style Dictation)

Dictator: William F. Fox, M.D.

Addressee: Miss Alice T. Knapp, 520 Greenleaf Circle, Asheville, NC 28804

Background: Dr. Fox is sending Miss Knapp some advice concerning her diet.

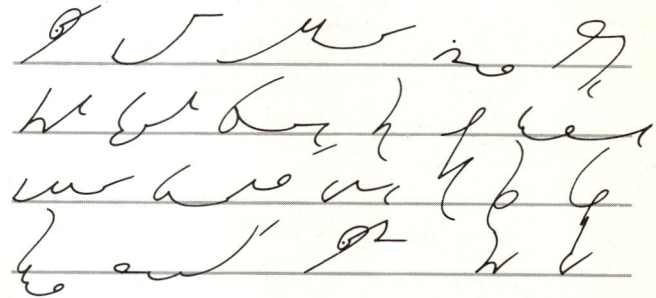

diet, kitchen, chocolate, hungry, dangerous, foods, pounds, balanced, group, vegetable, cereals, quart, poultry, citrus, grapefruit, breakfast, grocery, enriched, dietitian

Lesson 47

Page 146

(to be continued in Lesson 49-B)

47-C. Professional Language in Medicine

cholesterol (kə les′ tər ōl), n. a fatty, crystalline substance that is widely distributed in animal fats and tissues; important in metabolism.

dermatologist (dėr′ mə tol′ ə jist), n. a doctor who treats the skin and its diseases.

dietitian (dī′ ə tish′ ən), n. person trained to plan properly balanced food intakes.

lesion (lē′ zhən), n. abnormal change in the structure of an organ or tissue.

47-D. Communication in Medicine

Letter 1

Dictator: Donald Pelton, M. D.

BACKGROUND FOR COMMUNICATION #2. This memo to the new staff explains precontract relationships to prospective authors.

[shorthand notes]

pattern, precontract, prospectus, analysis, competitors, illustrations, thinks, desirable, guarantee

BACKGROUND FOR COMMUNICATION #3. This final communication discusses the procedures followed by the firm after it has received a prospectus or complete manuscript from an author. The memo will be dictated in office style.

LESSON 27

27-A. Effective Display Guidelines

MEMO STYLES. In Lesson 22 illustrations were given of various printed memo stationery styles, and you observed that some arrangements of introductory elements were more time consuming than others, either because of the number of elements and/or because of the positionings required in filling in the requested information. If the needed data can be supplied in a simple vertical form, the time of the transcriber is conserved.

Stationery for internal communication is designed primarily to (a) minimize transcribing time, (b) promote distribution speed, and (c) conserve reading time for the recipient. Attractive appearance from the point of view of vertically centering the message is disregarded. Attractiveness from the point of view of horizontal centering and neat appearance and readability are important just as in extraoffice letters. Neat corrections and adequate space breaks are no less important in memos than in extra-office letters. A secretary's reputation within the firm may be determined to a great extent by the quality of transcripts of internal communication.

27-B. Transcription Craftsmanship

HANDLING THE NOTEBOOK FOR NOTETAKING. The competent executive secretary uses her notetaking skills to speed the transformation of decisions into written form. The more unobtrusively she handles transcription the more quickly can the decision be transformed into typewritten form. She can handle the dictation unobtrusively not only by having a large shorthand vocabulary but also by the way in which she handles her notebook during dictation sessions.

The following suggestions will facilitate efficient notetaking:

1. Use a pen rather than a pencil. Pen-and-ink notes are easier to read. Take an extra pen with you in case one ceases to function.

2. Date the first page of each day's notes with the day, month, and year. Some stenographers place the date in the lower lefthand corner of the page for ease in locating a certain day's notes. Others who may begin a day's dictation on a partially filled page place the date at the beginning of the notes for that day.

3. Always leave a few lines blank at the beginning of each item for special instructions regarding number of copies to be made, order of transcription, special mailing directions, etc.

4. Write in longhand the names of individuals or firms if they are unfamiliar to you. The spellings of proper names

LESSON 47

47-A. System Control

[shorthand content]

47-B. THE OFFICE: A Decision-Making Center

[shorthand content]

vary so much that writing them in longhand is the only sure way of transcribing them accurately.

5. If the number of copies to be made is different from the usual requirement, make a notation about it above the shorthand notes for the memo or letter. It is discouraging and time-wasting to complete a transcript only to discover that additional copies were needed.

6. The ideal practice is for the stenographer to insert punctuation and paragraph marks as she takes dictation. This speeds up transcription and makes the copy more nearly accurate. Therefore, when time permits, insert all punctuation marks in the notes that you write.

7. If you take dictation from more than one person, put the initials of each beside or under the date where his dictation begins in your notebook.

8. Place a rubber band or paper clip in your notebook where the transcription should begin. A "finder" of this kind will help you start your work quickly.

9. Make some sort of distinguishing mark at the end of the notes for each memo or letter so that you can judge quickly the length of each transcript.

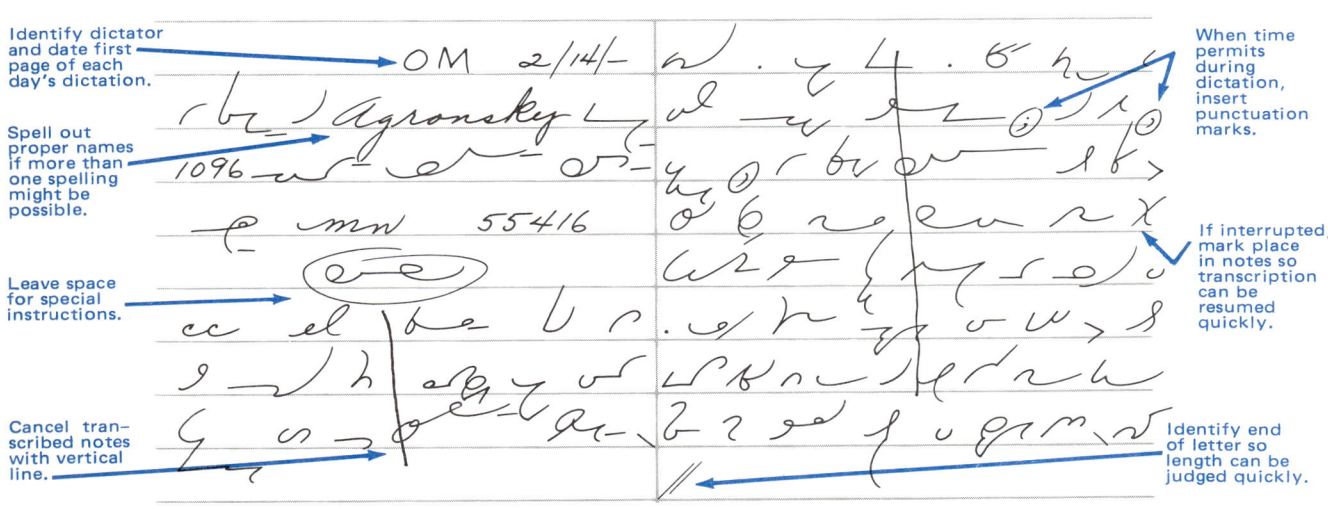

Handling the Notebook for Notetaking

Lesson 27

46-D. Proofreading Exercise

The letter on this page contains 25 errors in grammar, spelling, punctuation, word division, word choice, letter style, or typewriting. Type a copy of the material as it appears below. Begin the date on line 12 and use a one-inch left margin. Edit your typed copy, making the necessary corrections in pen or pencil.

June 31, 19--

Doctor Frank Reynolds
212 University Avenue
Pittsburg, PA   15214

Dear Frank

It is a pleasure to recomend Dr. Ralph Buttrey who is being considered for a position in your clinic. I have known Dr. Buttrey ever since he came east fourteen years ago to establish a practice in are community.

Ralph is a general practitioner par excellence. Dr. Buttrey is knowledgeable in many areas of medicine. On many occassions, he has taken time form an extremely busy schedule to participate in postgraduate seminars at various reputible schools of medicine. He also is an avid reader of professional literature and he keeps abreast of current research and trends in medicine. During his years in Racine, Ralph has served as president of the County Medical Society, as chief of staff at Racine Municipal Hospital, and as chairman of the Mental Health Board.

Dr. Buttrey was instrumental in instigating a community wide movement to attract new medical personnel to locate in our city. Primarly because of his efforts, Racine now has two additional pediatricians, a new surgeon, and another internist. Ralph told me recently that he is hopefull that three more general practitioners will soon come to Racine.

Dr. Butrey is active in community affairs. He is a member of Rotary, the Racine Chamber of Commerce, and the City Youth Advisory Board. He is a member of St. James Episcapol Church. Two years ago he was named "Racine Citizen of the Year".

Dr. Buttrey and his lovely wife have two boys and a girl, aged twelve, ten, and five, respectfully. He is devoted to his family and joins enthusiasticly in their frequent family camping trips.

I can insure you that Dr. Buttrey will be a fine addition to your staff, however, we will all be disappointed if he decides to leave Racine.

Sincerely Yours

Dr. Karl Finnen

kf   pl

27-C. Communication in Printing and Publishing

BACKGROUND FOR COMMUNICATIONS #1 AND #2. Your teacher will dictate two memos you practiced in Lesson 26, so your first transcription from your own notes will be on familiar dictation. Follow Memo Style 1, page i, in the Appendix.

BACKGROUND FOR COMMUNICATION #3. The Editorial Department wishes to encourage a new author to utilize illustrations in his manuscript. Use Memo Style 1.

27-D. Transcription Capsules

95
521-6404 16 104
100 (edt) 111
ellis johnson 117
6970 123
132
397-8402 138
146
154
1 (edt) 159
eg hanna 166
175
12:30 183
2:30 191
747-1121 199
3 (edt) 206
215
225
hertz 231
(397-4882) 240
8 (edt) 251
ama 262
8:30 268
(edt) 276

a allan peterson 280
10 (edt) 289
17 300
7 (edt) 310
ethan jones 315
320
18 331
10:30 342
(edt) 347
ama 352
1:30 361
(edt) 368
376
4:15 (edt) 382
388
o'hare 45 396
404
2^{50} 6:07 (edt) 410
o'hare 613 416
424
432
7:15 (pdt) 437
443
448

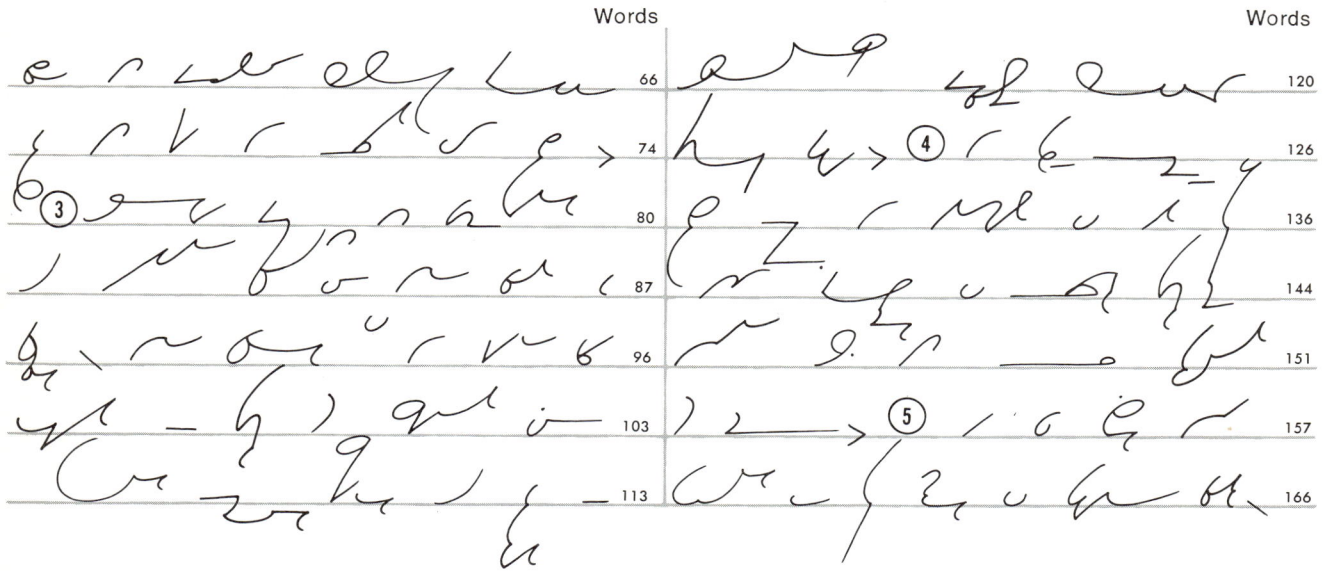

LESSON 28

28-A. System Control

These sentences are of the same dictation length as those in Lesson 26. Build automatization.

28-B. THE OFFICE: A Decision-Making Center

INSTRUCTIONS FOR THE ITINERARY. These shorthand notes were written as you organized the itinerary data that you had been accumulating in your trip folder. Transcribe them in suitable itinerary form. Use the format illustrated on page vi in the Appendix. Notice that telegraphic style is used to conserve space. Start your heading on Line 6. Use one-inch side margins. Single-space each entry and double-space between entries. Make one copy to serve as a dummy for a spirit master that you will prepare later.

28-C. Executive Language in Printing and Publishing

connotation (kon′ə tā′ shən), n. 1. the meaning of a word. 2. a second meaning suggested in addition to the simple definition.

inference (in′ fər əns), n. 1. act of inferring. 2. something which is inferred. 3. premises and conclusion.

overtone (ō′ vər tōn′), n. 1. a higher tone heard along with the fundamental tone. 2. a secondary quality or meaning.

28-D. Communication in Printing and Publishing

BACKGROUND FOR COMMUNICATION #1. The Executive Vice-President wishes to convey in writing his views on new product development to the President. This memo is the initial one, laying the foundation for more detailed comments in subsequent memos (in Lesson 30).

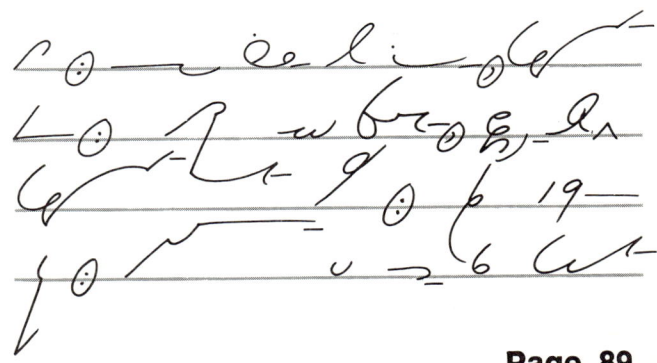

46-A. Signals in Written Communications

ENCLOSURE AND ATTACHMENT NOTATIONS. An enclosure notation is placed on a letter or memorandum when a statement is made within the message that one or more items are to be enclosed with it. This notation is made for two reasons: (1) it reminds the secretary or mailroom employee that one or more items are to be enclosed with the message, and (2) it alerts the addressee to the fact that one or more items should be enclosed with the incoming message.

If the message and enclosure are to be enclosed within an envelope, the enclosure notation is used. (The spelling *inclosure* is used in military correspondence.) If the message and enclosure are not to be enclosed within an envelope (an interoffice memorandum, for example), an attachment notation is sometimes used in place of the enclosure notation. In such case, the attachment is affixed securely to the message.

46-B. Transcription Craftsmanship

TIPS ON TYPING ENCLOSURE OR ATTACHMENT NOTATIONS. The enclosure or attachment notation is typed at the left margin a double space below the reference initials (or a double space below the closing lines, if there are no reference initials). Commonly used forms are included in the following example:

One enclosure:	PLT:SAM Enclosure	PLT:SAM Enc.	plt sam enc.	PLT:SAM Enclosure: Check	⎰ Leave a double space here.
More than one enclosure:	Enclosures	Encs.	encs.	Enclosures: Check Graph	
One attachment:	Attachment	Att.	attach.	Attachment: Check	
More than one attachment:	Attachments	Atts.	atts. (2)	Attachments: Check Graph	

46-C. Transcription Items

Background: Dr. W. A. Leff, your employer, is about to leave for Chicago to attend the American Medical Association convention. In this lesson you will transcribe his itinerary and two cover memorandums.

Instructions: Use Memorandum Style 2 shown on page i in the Appendix. Place an enclosure notation on Memorandum 1 and an attachment notation on Memorandum 2.

Memorandum 1

Words

[shorthand notation] 4
[shorthand notation] 10
[shorthand notation] 17

UNIT 9 — COMMUNICATION IN MEDICINE

BACKGROUND FOR COMMUNICATION #2. The Editor in Chief gives new authors some tips on kinds of copy to avoid.

sizeable, suspicious, ulterior, untoward, implication, uncomplimentary, racial, ethnic, derogatory, unintentionally

BACKGROUND FOR COMMUNICATION #3. This memo is in response to an inquiry about submitting manuscripts. It will be dictated in office style.

LESSON 29

29-A. Effective Display Guidelines

LETTER STYLES. In Lesson 17, readability factors, such as space breaks, size of margins, copy arrangement, and ribbon quality were discussed. Then in Lesson 19, appearance factors such as balance and "clean copy" were considered. In Lesson 24, stationery design was introduced as a factor in effective display of the written communication. Attention was called in Lesson 22 to desirable features in memo display style, and you transcribed several memos using one of the most efficient memo styles. Now in Lesson 29 you will be concerned with letter styles.

45-D. Proofreading Exercise

The memorandum on this page contains 25 errors in grammar, spelling, punctuation, word division, word choice, memorandum style, or typewriting. Type a copy of the material as it appears in this exercise; then edit your typed copy, making the necessary corrections in pen or pencil. Begin on line 9 and set a one-inch left margin.

MEMORANDUM

TO   : Members of the Company Recreation Comittee

FROM   : Paul Harder, Chairman

SUBJECT: Monthly Meeting

The Company Recreation Committee will meet in the Execetive Board Conference Room at 2:00 p.m., on Thursday, November 13. All members are urged to be present.

The major item on the agenda will be a discussion of the annual Christmas party. Some employees have expressed the opinion that this annual occurence should be discontinued. They beleive that, since the firm has become so large the party has become an impersonal affair, and has little meaning to those in attendance.

Some employees in the Maintainance Department have suggested that the money that has been apropriated for the Christmas party be used for some worth while community service project. (The amount allocated for this party is $2,000.00.

The suggestion has come from a member of the Personel Dept. that the Christmas party allocation be used to engage a "big name" performer to present a concert for employees and members of thier immediate families in the Company Audatorium.

Prior to our meeting on Wednesday, would you give some consideration to these questions.

1. Should the annual Christmas party be held in it's traditional form?

2. Should the Christmas party fund be used for some community service project?

3. If so, what kind of project.

4. Should the Christmas party fund be used for a performance of some kind to which employees and dependents might come?

           P.H.

ph sl

Lesson 45

In displaying messages going to persons outside the firm, some factors receive more emphasis than in displaying internal messages. Overall appearance receives more attention. The display style must be compatible with the design of the letterhead. Traditionally, the message has the "framed" look, as though it were a picture.

Letter styles are usually classified as "block" or "modified block." Impression on the recipient is a factor probably more important than what might be termed "typing efficiency." The letter style usually regarded as highest in "typing efficiency" is the block style, illustrated on page v in the Appendix. With all lines blocked at the left, there is no need to set tab stops or indentions. Its main limitations are: (1) less compatibility with "balanced" letterhead design than with "unbalanced," and (2) its lack of paragraph indentions, which might reduce readability. Various versions of the "modified block" style are compatible with most letterhead designs, and the version with paragraph indentions has the highest readability rating.

The letter style that perhaps would be rated highest in "typing efficiency" is the "simplified" version of the block style. In the "simplified" style, the salutation and complimentary close are omitted. None of the various "simplified" styles is widely used, possibly because they seem to lack the personal touch people are accustomed to in nonbusiness letters.

Punctuation styles also enter into effective display. These styles refer to punctuation used in opening and closing lines of extra-office letters. The style having the greatest "typing efficiency" is the "open" because no punctuation marks are used after the opening or closing lines of a letter.

The style most commonly used (and not noticeably less efficient) is the "mixed," which differs from the open only in having a colon after the salutation and a comma after the complimentary close.

The transcriber can "mix and match" letter and punctuation styles to suit the message situation.

29-B. Transcription Craftsmanship

HANDLING THE NOTEBOOK FOR TRANSCRIPTION. In Lesson 27, you learned some techniques for handling the notebook that would assist you in notetaking. There are also some techniques for handling the notebook in transcribing that will enable you to transcribe most efficiently.

1. Check through your notes for any rush items that should be given precedence.

2. Check the beginning of your notes for each communication before starting to transcribe to see whether extra carbon copies are to be made or whether special mailing instructions are to be followed.

3. If information is to be obtained or facts checked before completing the transcript, do that before beginning transcription. Such information might change the content or setup used.

4. Estimate length of the transcript so that you can choose appropriate writing line length. Such lines as subject and attention, quoted matter, and tabulations have the effect of increasing the length of the transcript.

5. Read in thought phrases so you will have to read your notes only once. This will insure your not misreading an outline.

6. Upon completing a transcript, strike a vertical line through the notes to indicate they have been transcribed.

7. If transcription is interrupted by a telephone call or by someone coming by your desk, quickly make a checkmark at the point where you are in your notes

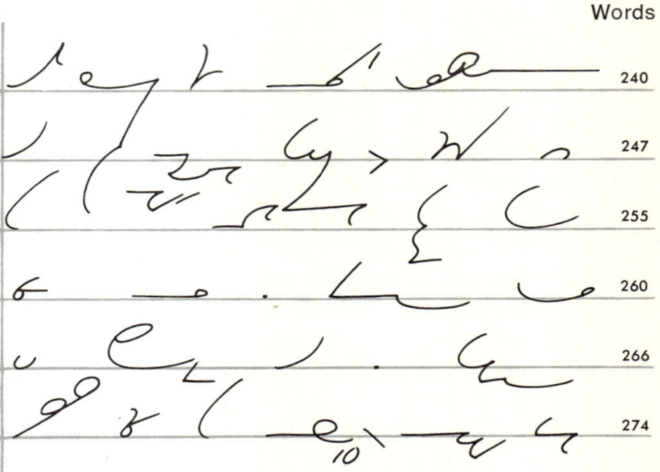

Letter 2
(to be dictated)

Dictator: Hugh McCarthy, Sales Manager, Regal Cruises

Addressee: Mr. and Mrs. Joseph Bradley, St. Francis Hotel, 335 Powell Street, San Francisco, CA 94102

Background: Mr. McCarthy wants to interest Mr. and Mrs. Bradley in a cruise to Mexico.

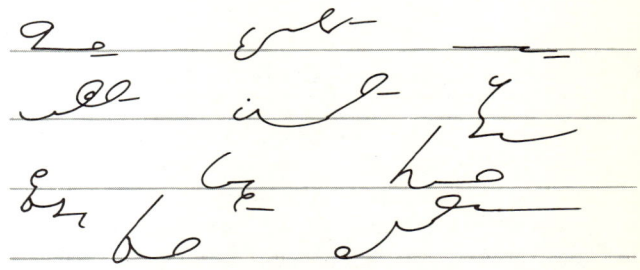

Acme, Southwest, Mexican, Riviera, holiday, optional, excursions, Princess, gourmet, gala, entertainment

Letter 3
(to be dictated)

Dictator: Ruth Warnke, Travel Agent, Tourist Travel, Inc.

Addressee: Mr. and Mrs. Warren Weaver, Hotel Berliner, 113 Kurfurstendamm, Berlin, Germany

Background: Miss Warnke wants to inform the Weavers, traveling in Europe, that there has been a change in their itinerary.

so that you can resume transcription quickly. A red pencil mark will be easily visible.

8. Type the envelope for a letter before going to the next transcript. Attach enclosures securely.

9. Place the envelope at the top of the letter, face up, with the flap hooked over the letter. With both the envelope address and inside address visible, the danger of sending a letter in the wrong envelope will be minimized.

10. Place finished transcripts face down on your desk or in a tray in a desk drawer so that no one passing your desk will be tempted to read the correspondence.

11. Follow the practice of your firm in handling file copies. Sometimes the secretary retains them until the originals have been mailed; sometimes the file copies are put in the outgoing mailbox and taken by the mail messenger to the Filing Department.

12. Filled notebooks should be handled according to the firm's practices. Some firms have them dated on the front and filed for a specified length of time. Other firms have them destroyed immediately.

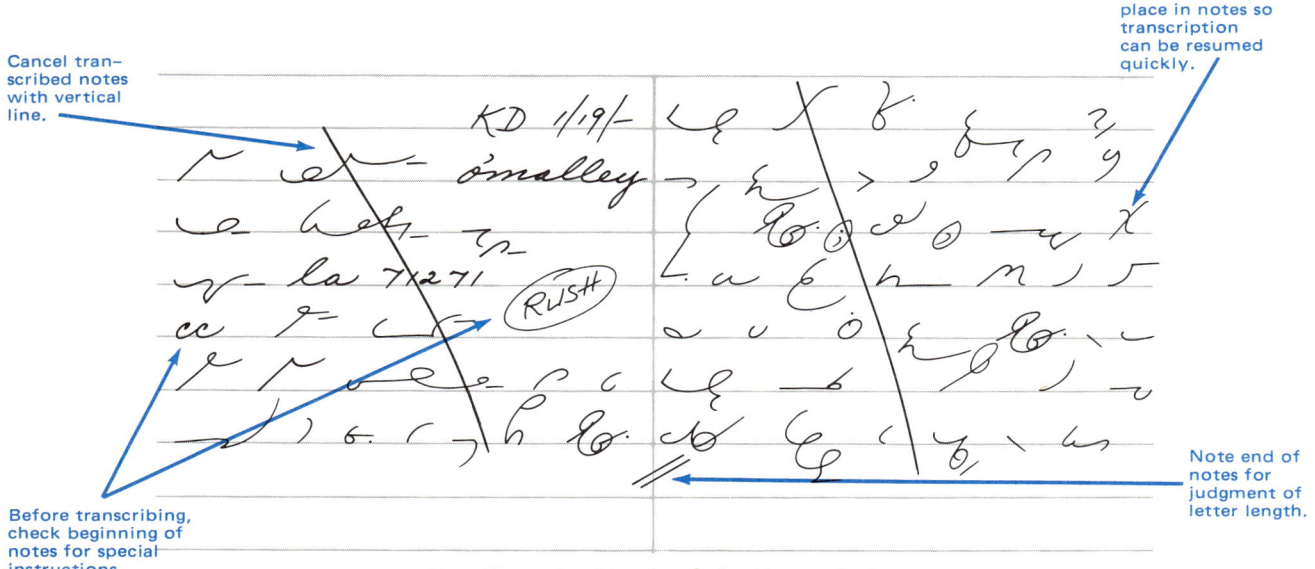

Handling the Notebook in Transcription

29-C. Communication in Printing and Publishing

BACKGROUND FOR COMMUNICATIONS #1 AND #2. You will take from dictation two of the memos that you practiced in Lesson 28. Use Memo Style 1, which is illustrated on page i in the Appendix.

BACKGROUND FOR COMMUNICATION #3. The Editor in Chief dictates a memo to be sent to the Manuscript Committee along with material which has been submitted by an author for publication, so that they might examine it.

LESSON 45

45-A. Signals in Written Communications

MAILING NOTATIONS. The notation PERSONAL is typed on an envelope bearing a business address when the sender wishes to have the message delivered to the addressee unopened. If the sender wishes to indicate that the contents of a message are personal or confidential, the notation PERSONAL or CONFIDENTIAL should also be typed on the letter.

When the writer sends a message to an individual who may not yet have arrived at the address typed on the envelope, the notation HOLD FOR ARRIVAL should be placed on the envelope. When the writer sends a message to an individual who may no longer be at the address given on the envelope, the notation PLEASE FORWARD should be placed on the envelope.

45-B. Transcription Craftsmanship

TIPS ON TYPING SIGNALS FOR MAILING. The notations PERSONAL, CONFIDENTIAL, HOLD FOR ARRIVAL, and PLEASE FORWARD should be typed on the envelope a triple space below the return address and three spaces from the left edge of the envelope. Such notations should not extend into the OCR reading zone of the envelope. These notations may either be underlined or typed in all capitals. If the notations PERSONAL or CONFIDENTIAL are typed on a letter, they are placed three or four line spaces above the inside address. Such notations should either be underlined or typed in all capitals.

45-C. Transcription Letters

Instructions: Use modified block style with indented paragraphs and mixed punctuation. Use the following mailing notations on the letters indicated:

    Letter 1—PERSONAL
    Letter 2—Hold for Arrival
    Letter 3—PLEASE FORWARD

        Letter 1

Dictator: (Miss) Alice T. Winters, Chairman, City Recreation Director Selection Committee

Addressee: Martin P. Lynch, Recreation Supervisor, Bakersfield City Hall, 1501 Truxtun Avenue, Bakersfield, CA 93301

Background: Miss Winters is inviting Mr. Lynch to apply for the position of City Recreation Director, which is open in Salem.

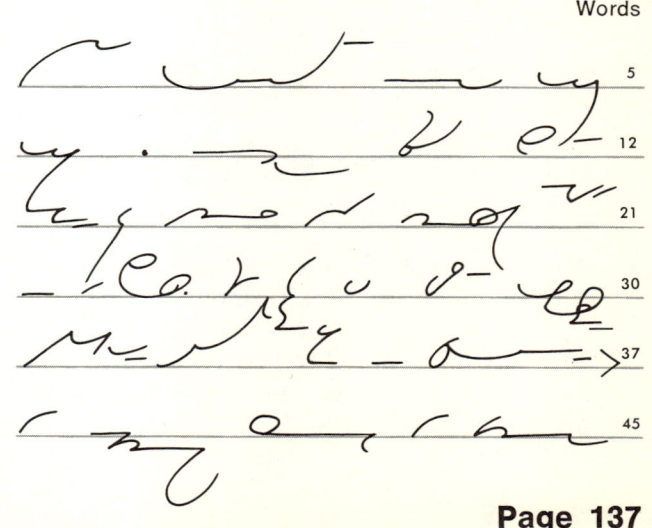

29-D. Transcription Capsules

Lesson 29

Letter 2
(Office-Style Dictation)

Dictator: Clinton C. Young, City Councilman

Addressee: John McDonald, President, Omaha Rodeo Association, 4320 Parkview Road, Omaha, NE 68128

Background: Mr. Young is writing for information that will be helpful to the City Council members as they consider whether or not to permit a rodeo to be held in Metropolitan Stadium in Omaha.

Metropolitan, Stadium, rodeo, semiannual, Council, presiding, projected, attendants, concessions, beverages

Lesson 44 Page 136

LESSON 30

30-A. System Control

The sentences are of the same dictation length as those in 26-A and 28-A.

30-B. THE OFFICE: A Decision-Making Center

(to be continued in Lesson 47)

44-C. Executive Language in Entertainment and Recreation

booking (bu̇k′ ing), n. a contract, engagement, or scheduled performance of an entertainer.

combo (kom′ bō), n. a small jazz or dance band.

rathskeller (räts′ kel′ ər), n. a restaurant, usually located below street level.

44-D. Communication in Entertainment and Recreation

Letter 1

Dictator: Edward Carlson, Booking Agent, Carlson Entertainment Agency

Addressee: T. L. Coleman, Manager, Alpine Lodge Rathskeller, 1121 Alpine Street, Worcester, MA 01610

Background: Mr. Carlson is soliciting bookings for a combo called the Robin Hoods.

[Shorthand text]

Outgoing Airmail Schedule

Depart Local P.O.	Destination	Via Flight	Arrive Destination
6:30 AM	Dallas	BN-167	7:50 AM
"	New York	"	12:58 PM
"	Austin	"	9:42 AM
"	San Antonio	"	9:11 AM
"	Houston	"	9:47 AM
"	Dallas	CO-180	7:50 AM
"	El Paso	CO-181	8:15 AM
"	Phoenix	"	8:34 AM
"	Los Angeles	"	9:20 AM
"	Wichita Falls	CO-190	9:25 AM
"	Lawton, OK	"	9:57 AM
"	Oklahoma City	"	10:31 AM
"	Tulsa	"	11:12 AM
"	Kansas City	"	12:10 AM
9:05 AM	Midland	CO-142	10:13 AM
"	Clovia	TT-625	9:50 AM
"	Santa Fe	"	10:53 AM
"	Albuquerque	"	11:23 AM
"	Dallas	CO-198	11:15 AM
"	Dallas	BN-165	11:29 AM
"	San Antonio	"	12:51 PM
"	Kansas City, MO	"	1:38 PM
"	Houston	"	12:47 PM
"	Corpus Christi	"	1:51 PM
11:50 AM	Dallas	CO-192	1:25 PM
"	Albuquerque	CO-153	12:46 PM
"	San Francisco	"	5:10 PM
"	Colorado Springs	"	1:57 PM
"	Denver	"	2:35 PM
"	Dallas	BN-271	1:49 PM
"	Austin	"	2:57 PM
"	El Paso	CO-111	2:00 PM
"	Los Angeles	"	3:50 PM
"	Houston	TT-331	4:59 PM
"	Austin	"	4:10 PM

Outgoing Airmail Schedule

▶ 30-C. Executive Language in Printing and Publishing

exotic (eg zot′ik), *adj.* **1.** introduced from another country; not native. **2.** strikingly unusual.

inhibit (in hib′it), *v.* **1.** to prohibit or forbid from doing something. **2.** to restrain or repress; hinder.

peer (pir), *n.* **1.** person who is of equal standing with another. **2.** one who has a title; great by birth or rank.

[Shorthand text]

▶ 30-D. Communication in Printing and Publishing

BACKGROUND FOR COMMUNICATION #1. In this memo, the Executive Vice-President expands on the topic of market research, which he mentioned in his memo on new product development (Lesson 28).

[Shorthand text]

LESSON 44

44-A. System Control

[Shorthand notes]

44-B. THE OFFICE: A Decision-Making Center

[Shorthand notes]

BACKGROUND FOR COMMUNICATION #2. Mr. Barnes explains his point of view regarding product acquisition, product processing, and product distribution.

centralized, sharper, unmistakably, belabor, substantially, intellectual, disproportionate, rationing, conventional, penetrating, experimental, foolproof

BACKGROUND FOR COMMUNICATION #3. In this memo, Mr. Barnes lists the factors that must be considered if the firm is to move in the direction of new product development. It will be dictated in office style.

43-D. Proofreading Exercise

The letter below contains 25 errors in grammer, spelling, punctuation, word division, word choice, letter style, or typewriting. Type the letter as shown, beginning the date on line 12 and using a one-inch left margin; then edit your typed copy, making the necessary corrections in pen or pencil. You may wish to review the proofreading tips in Lessons 32 and 34 before beginning.

January 12, 19--

Dr. Edward Gates, M.D.
5119 Carter St.
Miami, FL   33133

Dear Dr. Gates:

The Miami Dinner Club, Inc. would like to invite you to join the ranks of its many members, who enjoy the privilige of ordering two dinners for the price of one. These individuals dine in recomended restaurants and supper clubs. They enjoy any gourmet selection on the menu.

How does the Dinner Club operate? You simply buy a book of twelve coupons for $15.00. Each coupon entitles you to a free meal in each of a dozen fine restaurants in the Miami area. You may select any dinner you wish from the menu at the regular price and your dinning companion may order a meal of comparable value at no cost with a coupon.

The coupons may be used any evening from Sunday through Thursday. There is no restriction as to the number of coupons that you may use during any single week or month. The coupons must be used however within a 12 month period. The use of the coupons are not limited to the purchaser of the book and his guest. Any one may use them. Thus, you may share them with friends if you wish.

These coupon books will be available only through the current month. May I suggest that you place your order for one immediately. Just complete the enclosed postal card, and drop in it the mail box. We will send you the coupon book at once and bill you.

Should you have further questions about the Miami Dinner Club you may call us at L03-9960.

We hope that you will soon be entertaining your friends at some of the exclusive eating accomodations in Miami at a fraction of the cost you would usually pay.

Respectively yours

(Mrs.) Norma Phillips
Sales Represenative

np rh

LESSON 31

31-A. System Control

The sentences are of the same dictation length as those in Lesson 30.

① ② ③ ④ ⑤

31-B. THE OFFICE: A Decision-Making Center

Addressee: Mr. and Mrs. Marshall C. Perkins, 1121 East Anne, Phoenix AZ 85040

Background: The Canton City Recreation Supervisor is writing to Mr. and Mrs. Perkins, who are at their winter home in Arizona, to thank them for their contribution to the city recreation program.

Instructions: Use modified block style with indented paragraphs and mixed punctuation. Place the date at the right margin. Send the letter airmail. Type a mailing notation on the letter and envelope.

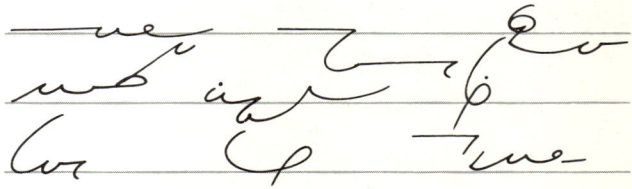

memorial, improvements, cyclone, tornado, horizontal, behalf, bronze, plaque, McQuarrie

Letter 3
(to be dictated)

Dictator: Patrick M. Kelly, Director, Colorado Parks Commission

Background: This form letter will be sent to prospective campers to inform them of two new camping sites available to the public.

Instructions: Prepare a double-spaced draft of this form letter for Mr. Kelly. No inside address will be used. Type the usual closing lines. Mr. Kelly will sign his name on the offset master.

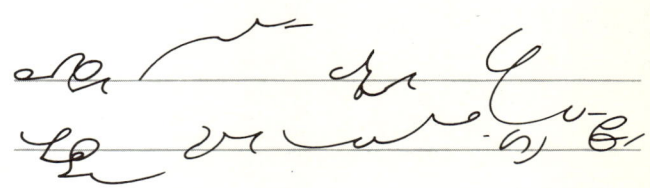

enthusiasts, Denver, outskirts, Pueblo, recreational, showers, laundry, successive, assigned

Letter 2
(to be dictated)

Dictator: Brooks L. Carpenter, Recreation Supervisor

Lesson 43   Page 132

31-C. Executive Language in Insurance

contention (kən ten′ shən), n. 1. verbal argument or dispute. 2. statement put forth in an argument.

deposition (dep′ əz ish′ ən), n. 1. act of removing from high office. 2. testimony under oath.

reinsurance (re in shŭr′ əns), n. 1. insuring again. 2. transfer of a risk already covered under an existing contract.

31-D. Communication in Insurance

BACKGROUND FOR COMMUNICATION #1. Prior to this date the University has not carried liability insurance for athletic and other events held in the City Auditorium or Coliseum. Because of the filing of a damage suit in connection with an accident during a basketball game, the administration has decided that liability insurance must be carried on future events.

LESSON 43

43-A. Signals in Written Communications

AIRMAIL AND SPECIAL DELIVERY NOTATIONS. The secretary must often determine whether to mail a message first class, airmail, special delivery, or whether to use a combination of these services. To make a wise choice, she must consider the urgency of the message, the geographical location of the recipient, and the day on which the message will probably be delivered. There may be no advantage, for example, to use the more costly airmail or special delivery service for a message sent to a recipient who lives in a nearby location and who receives an early morning mail delivery. When messages are sent to certain distant locations on a Thursday or Friday, there may be little reason for using airmail service. In such instances, both the first-class and the airmail messages would likely be delivered the following Monday. Good judgment must dictate in what manner such messages should be sent.

43-B. Transcription Craftsmanship

TIPS ON TYPING MAILING SIGNALS. The U.S. Postal Service requests that AIRMAIL and/or SPECIAL DELIVERY notations be typed on an envelope just below the stamp position and at least three line spaces above the address. These notations may also be typed on the letter in all caps a double space above the inside address. Mailing notations are placed on letters for record purposes. When first-class mailing service is desired, no notation is made on the letter or the envelope. Notice that AIRMAIL is typed as one word on business correspondence.

Airmail Notation on Letter

Airmail Notation on Envelope

43-C. Transcription Letters

Letter 1

Dictator: Gordon Mitchell, Principal, North High School.

Addressee: Frederick C. Williamson, Principal, Mann Senior High School, Buffalo NY 14202

Background: North High School officials are considering the feasibility of installing synthetic turf in their stadium. This letter is written by Mr. Mitchell to seek information about such turf from Mr. Williamson.

Instructions: When typing this letter, use a modified block style with indented paragraphs and mixed punctuation. Place the date at the right margin. Send the letter airmail special delivery. Type mailing notations on both the letter and the envelope.

BACKGROUND FOR COMMUNICATION #2. This memo explains in detail the responsibilities of persons in charge of conferences, etc., in seeing that the proper liability insurance is arranged for.

statutory, necessitate, premises, henceforth, participants, tuition, premium, regardless, budget, coverage

BACKGROUND FOR COMMUNICATION #3. Charles B. Block reports to the Secretary and General Counsel of the insurance firm that a deposition has been taken from Mrs. Larsen, who has been seeking settlement in a suit brought against the insurance firm. It will be dictated in office style.

LESSON 32

32-A. Efficient Dispatch of Communications

DISTRIBUTION MEDIA FOR MEMOS. Interoffice memos may be sent to the addressees by various media. One medium for dispatching memos to offices within the same building is the messenger or mail clerk. A firm using this medium would have a scheduled route and time plan. When distribution is by hand, various methods of indicating recipients are available.

If several people are to read a memo and time is not a deciding factor, one copy of a memo may be circulated to the recipients through attaching a routing slip to the memo on which is listed the names of those who are to read it. The first person receiving the memo reads it, checks his name

42-D. Communication in Entertainment and Recreation

Letter 1

Dictator: Paul L. Taylor, President, Community Concert Association

Addressee: George A. Wilson, 1101 Morningside Drive, Lincoln, NE 68506

Background: This letter is written to Mr. Wilson, a member of the Community Concert Association Executive Board, to inform him about an impending meeting of the Board.

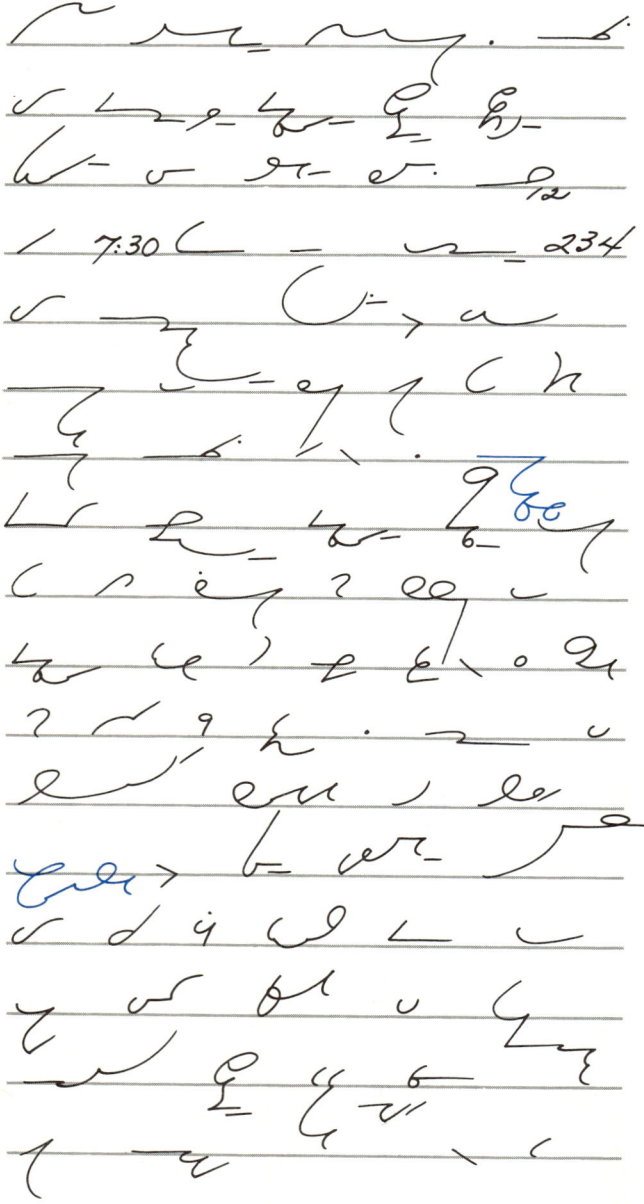

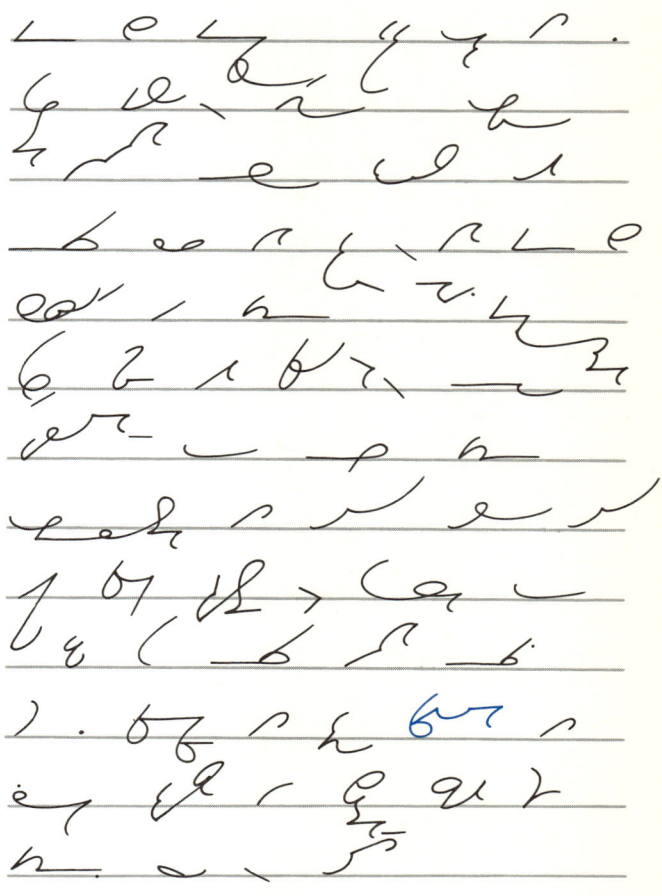

Letter 2
(to be dictated)

Dictator: Doris T. Palmer, President, Eastern Recreation Directors Association

Addressee: Members of the Eastern Recreation Directors Association

Background: This form letter will be sent to ERDA members to give them preliminary information about their annual convention.

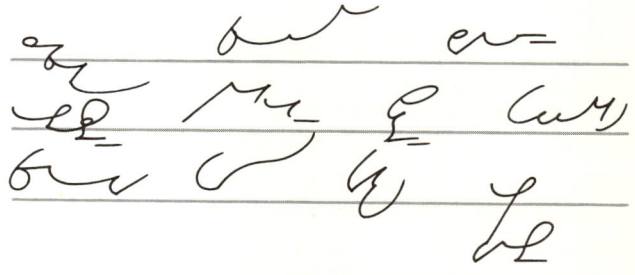

encircle, calendar, Eastern, Recreation, Directors, Association, provocative, panelist, pertinent, participant, registration on the routing slip, and puts it in the outgoing mail to be picked up and delivered to the next person on the list. A routing slip is illustrated below.

Routing Slip

If the message needs to be read as soon as possible by all addressees, then a copy is made for each person concerned. When this procedure is followed, the list of names may be typed on the memo and a different name checked on each copy to guide the messenger in distributing the copy. See the illustration shown below.

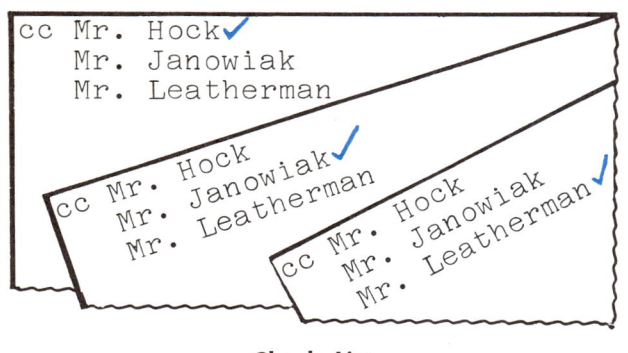

Check List

Whether or not a memo is placed in an envelope is determined by the confidentiality of the message, by whether there are attachments that might become separated if not placed in an envelope, or by whether the material is a final draft to be mailed subsequently to someone outside the firm.

Different sizes and types of envelopes are available for internal communications. Some envelopes, such as the No. 10, require the memo to be folded. Other envelopes, such as the 9½ by 12½, permit the memo to be delivered unfolded.

Usually, envelopes for interoffice communications are made of kraft or manila paper. Holes are sometimes spaced out down the middle of the envelope so that the secretary quickly detects whether anything has been overlooked in emptying the envelope. Chain envelopes and one-time envelopes are shown below.

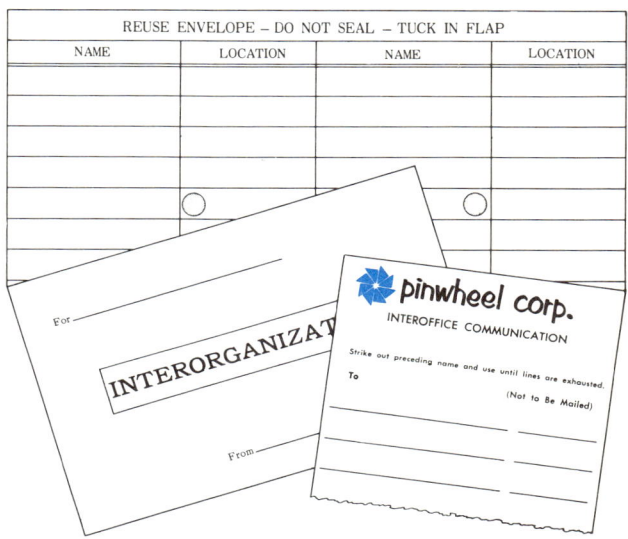

Interoffice Envelopes

Those that are to be used more than once usually have ruled lines on the face. The name of the person who is to receive the memo is written on the first unused line. The envelope is not sealed unless the material is confidential. When the addressee receives the envelope, he draws a line through his name; and the secretary saves the envelope to be used in sending a memo later to someone else.

When memos are sent to different buildings within a city, the memos are usually placed in envelopes for protection. Interbranch, interorganizational, and interdivisional memos sent between offices in different cities are usually collected by the mailing department, put together in one envelope, and dispatched once a day via the United States mails.

42-C. Executive Language

impresario (im' prə sä' re ō), n. 1. one who organizes or sponsors an entertainment. 2. producer; manager.

patron (pā' trən), n. 1. person chosen as a special guardian or supporter. 2. regular client or customer of an establishment. 3. wealthy supporter of an artist or artistic endeavor; social or financial sponsor of entertainment.

repertoire (rep' ər twär), n. the works an artist or entertainer is prepared to perform.

32-B. Transcription Craftsmanship

PROOFREADING TECHNIQUES. The transcriber is responsible for the accuracy of the transcript. She has the responsibility of proofreading her work.

To be sure that no errors are overlooked, the transcriber must read for thought—not just scan the copy. Certain kinds of errors cannot be detected unless one has read for thought. Some examples of such errors are: *of* for *on*, *then* for *than*; the omission of a word, a line, a sentence, or even a paragraph.

A transcriber does not know she has made a typographical error unless she breaks her rhythm when she makes the error. Transpositions are sometimes made without a break in rhythm; letters or words can be omitted without a break in rhythm. Thus, the only way to be sure of 100 percent correct copy is to proofread carefully.

Copy should be read while the transcript is still in the machine so that, if an error is found, it can be corrected without losing the time involved in reinserting and realigning horizontally and vertically.

Some expert transcribers proofread each paragraph as soon as it is typed rather than waiting until the page has been completed. The advantages of this procedure are:

1. If the ink has not had time to soak into the paper, the impression is more easily removed.

2. There is less trouble from slippage if the papers in the machine do not have to be rolled very far to reach the error.

3. There is less likelihood of roller marks on carbon copies if rolling the papers backward and forward is kept at a minimum.

4. If an uncorrectable error is detected, the transcriber can start over at once without the loss of time that would be involved if she had completed the entire page and then proofread.

32-C. Communication in Insurance

BACKGROUND FOR COMMUNICATIONS #1 AND #2. The memos to be transcribed are #1 and #2 that you practiced in Lesson 31. Your transcription, then, will be from your own notes taken on familiar material.

DIRECTIONS FOR TRANSCRIPTION. Use Memo Style 1, illustrated on page i in the Appendix, for your transcription.

BACKGROUND FOR COMMUNICATION #3. A field agent for an insurance company has written to the home office to see whether coverage on residence fixed glass should be attached to the policy before the building of the residence is completed. This memo replies to the query.

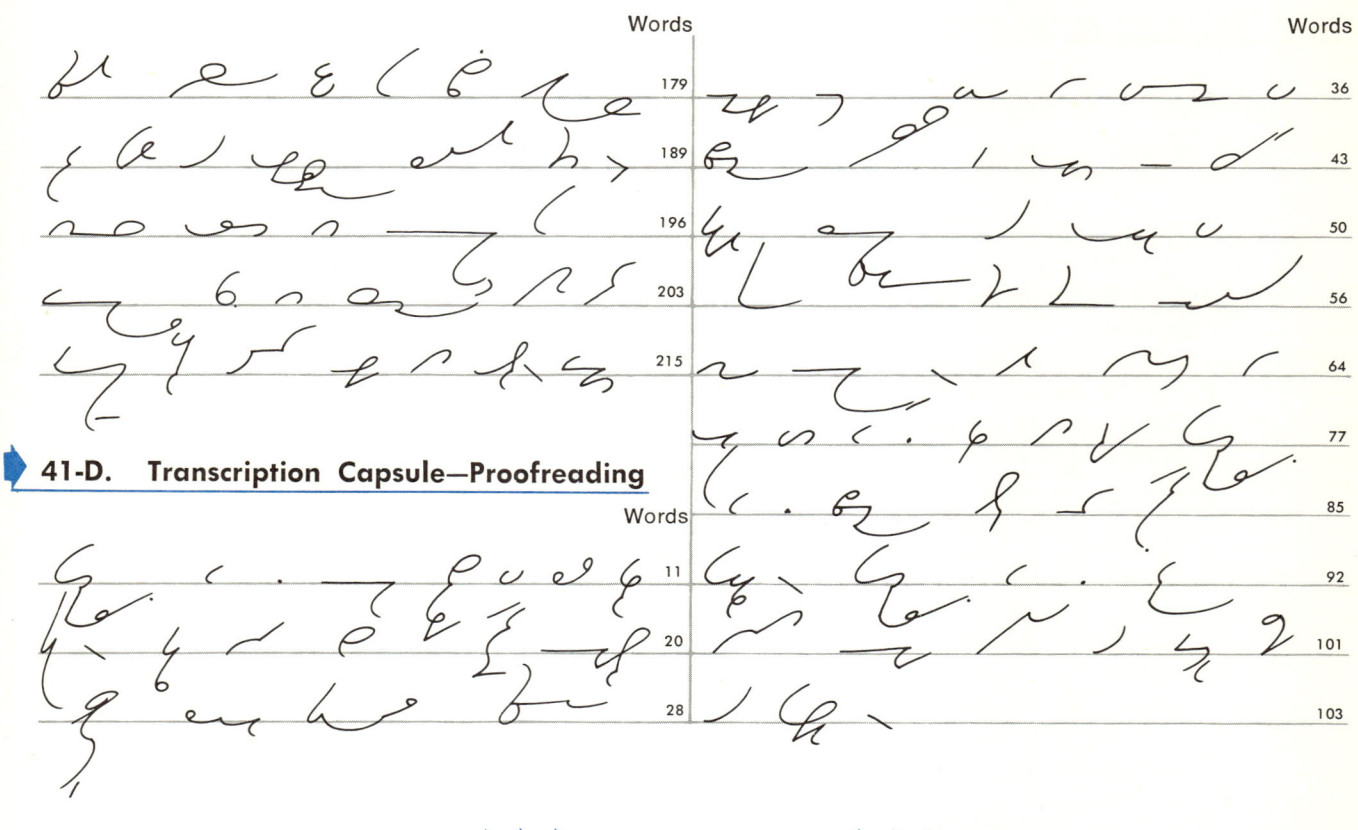

▶ 41-D. Transcription Capsule—Proofreading

▶▶▶ LESSON 42 ◀◀◀

▶ 42-A. System Control

▶ 42-B. THE OFFICE: A Decision-Making Center

Lesson 42

Page 128

32-D. Transcription Capsules

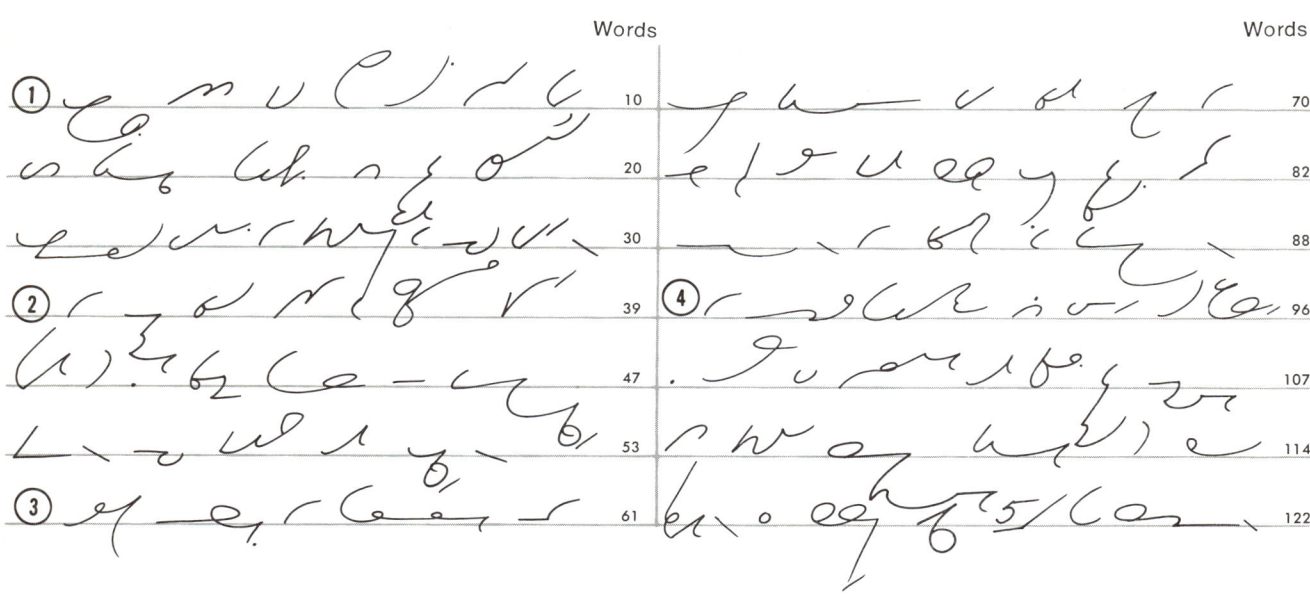

LESSON 33

33-A. System Control

The sentences are of the same dictation length as those in 30-A.

33-B. THE OFFICE: A Decision-Making Center

Lesson 33

Page 102

is informing a member about the facilities in the refurbished building.

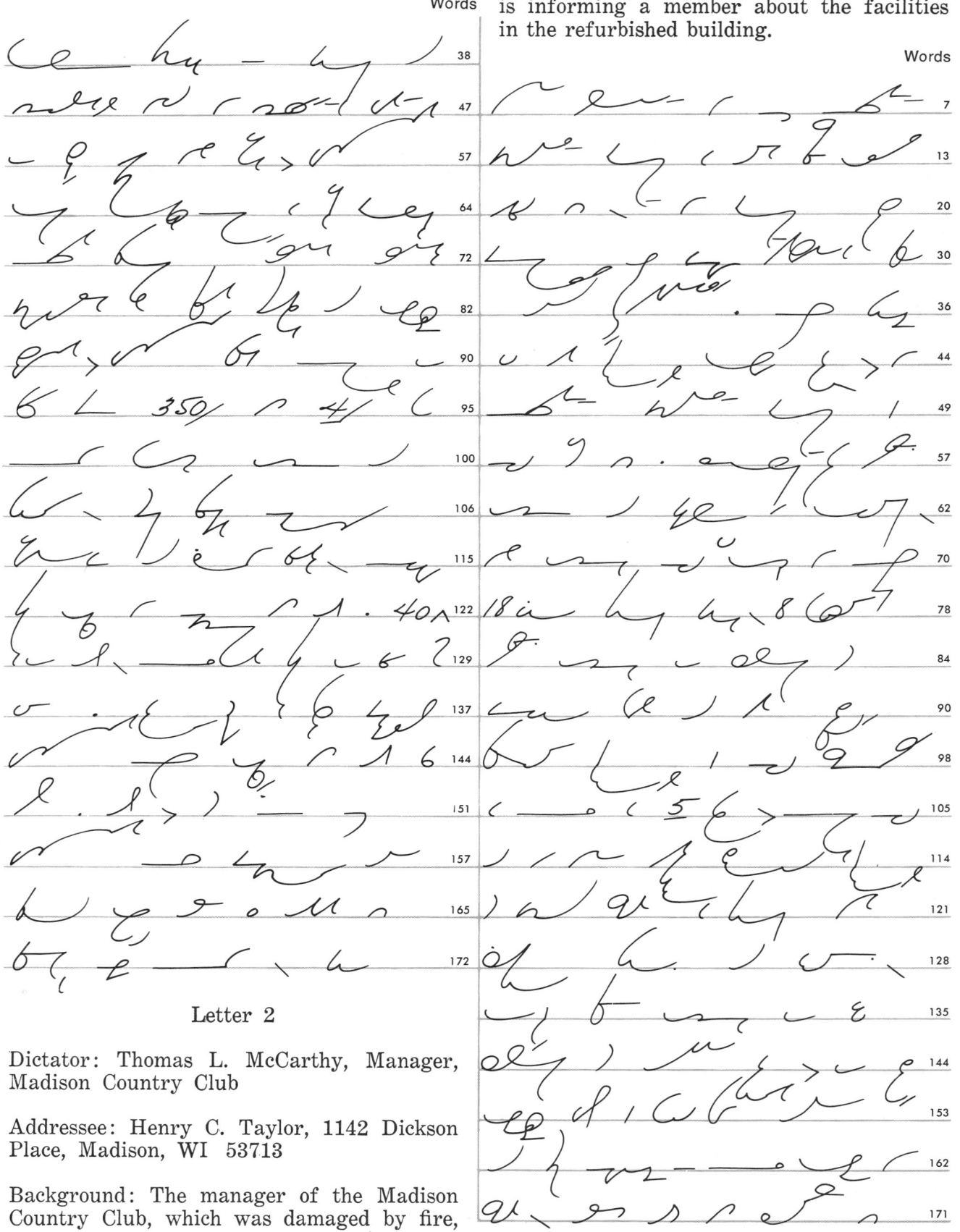

Letter 2

Dictator: Thomas L. McCarthy, Manager, Madison Country Club

Addressee: Henry C. Taylor, 1142 Dickson Place, Madison, WI 53713

Background: The manager of the Madison Country Club, which was damaged by fire,

33-C. Executive Language in Insurance

annuitant (ə nū′ ə tənt), n. person qualified to receive an annuity.

commuted value, n. sum of money necessary to provide future payments as provided for in an annuity policy.

insurant, (in shur′ ənt), n. person who is insured.

LESSON 41

41-A. Codes in Written Communications

REFERENCE INITIALS. Reference initials are used in correspondence to pinpoint responsibility. They identify the dictator and the transcriber. Such initials serve as an important control measure in offices where there are many dictators and transcribers. Various patterns are used in typing reference initials, and a secretary should discuss with her employer the style that would be most suitable for use in their office.

41-B. Transcription Craftsmanship

You may wish to use the following commonly accepted practices when you type reference initials:

1. Type the reference initials at the left margin a double space below the closing lines of a letter.

2. Type the reference initials a double space below the last line of the body of a memorandum.

3. Use only your initials when the dictator's name is typed in the closing lines of a letter.

4. When the dictator's name does not appear in the closing lines, type both his and your initials. (example: JAG:tld, jag/tld, jag tld)

5. When a letter is signed by someone other than the dictator, type the initials of the dictator and then your initials.

6. If the signer wishes to disguise the fact that a letter was dictated by another person you may type a three-letter code consisting of the last initials of the dictator, the transcriber, and the signer. (Example: The code *stl* might designate Smith, the dictator; Thompson, the transcriber; and Larson, the signer.)

7. The use of lower case initials with a diagonal or a space between the sets of reference initials simplifies their typing. The use of the shift key for capital letters or the colon can be avoided. (Example: jag/tld or jag tld)

41-C. Transcription Letters

In Transcription Letters 1 and 2 use a modified block style, illustrated on page v of the Appendix, with indented paragraphs and mixed punctuation. Place the date at the right margin.

Letter 1

Dictator: James A. Bailey, Director, National Park Commission

Addressee: Paul C. Miller, Director, Placement Bureau, Western College, Las Vegas, NV 89101

Background: This letter is to inform the Western College Placement Bureau of summer employment opportunities in national parks for students.

UNIT 8 — COMMUNICATION IN ENTERTAINMENT & RECREATION

33-D. Communication in Insurance

BACKGROUND FOR COMMUNICATION #1. The Underwriting Department in the Home Office is explaining in writing to its agents the rule now in effect with regard to issuing policies to applicants who may present a hazard from military or naval service.

BACKGROUND FOR COMMUNICATION #2. This communication interprets for the Company representatives the provisions found in the *Application for Change of Beneficiary for One-Sum Settlement*.

annuity, accidental, remainder, guaranteed, beneficiaries, executors, administrators, legally, guardian, deemed

BACKGROUND FOR COMMUNICATION #3. The Home Office is advising its representatives of the new commission rates for Annually Renewable Term (ART) Policies and Riders. The memo will be dictated in office style.

Secretaries must possess more than good basic skills

... in order to perform the stenographic portion of their work effectively. They must have the ability to think through stenographic problems and to use methods and procedures that will enable them to process data efficiently. They must be able to follow instructions precisely. They must have a knowledge of the specialized vocabulary in the industry or profession in which they work.

Secretaries must be able to set up many types of business communications in acceptable form. They must establish a proofreading routine that will enable them to spot any errors in their work. Finally, they must be able to transcribe many kinds of dictated problems in a reasonable period of time.

Now that you have developed a basic skill in recording and transcribing dictation, you should have two goals as you continue this course: (1) to build your recording and transcribing rates to a level that meets the demands of business and (2) to develop further the concomitant knowledge and skills that secretaries need as they perform the stenographic phase of their work.

In the second half of this textbook, you will have the opportunity to continue to develop your shorthand recording skill. Two lessons in each of the next six units will be devoted to activities that should help you gain speed in recording shorthand dictation and in reading from shorthand notes. As you read from well-written shorthand plates in these lessons, you will also be reviewing administrative management principles in such areas as records management; office layout; work simplification; duplicating processes; and methods, procedures, and systems.

In Units 9 through 14, you will have many opportunities to continue to develop your transcription skill. Three lessons in each of these units will contain a variety of business communication problems, including business letters and memorandums with special lines and multiple copies, message-and-reply forms, news releases, minutes of meetings, reports, speeches, and itineraries. Some of these problems will be dictated to you in office style.

In the units that follow, you will continue to develop your basic shorthand vocabulary. Each of the 1,500 most commonly used words in business correspondence is repeated in the ensuing lessons. Each of the Speedforms is also repeated in this section of the text.

In the units ahead, you will have a chance to extend your shorthand vocabulary. By the time you complete the lessons in this textbook, you will have encountered each of the 5,000 most commonly used words in business correspondence. In Units 9 through 16, you will also be exposed to specialized vocabulary in the areas of recreation, medicine, transportation, mass media, public administration, and banking.

As you continue the lessons in this textbook, you will have additional opportunities to apply each of the punctuation principles that appear on page viii of the Appendix. A series of proofreading letters will give you a chance to develop proofreading skill.

Units 15 and 16 contain two week-long simulation projects. These culminating activities will give you an opportunity to apply the stenographic knowledge and skills that you have developed throughout the course. In one project, you will serve as secretary to the chairman of the Department of Office Administration of Western University. In the second project, you will be employed as secretary to the president of the Carter Employment Service.

LESSON 34

34-A. Efficient Dispatch of Communications

DISTRIBUTION MEDIA FOR EXTERNAL COMMUNICATIONS. The outlet for external communications is, of course, the United States mail. As was mentioned in Lesson 30, the executive secretary should have a copy of the schedule of mail delivery from the Mailing Department to the Main Post Office and a copy of the mail departure schedule from the Main Post Office. Knowing these time schedules could make a difference of a half day or a full day in travel time.

Regular mail is assumed to go by surface transportation, i.e., mail truck, bus, or railway. Usually a destination less than 300 miles away from the sending office is reached as quickly by regular mail as by airmail.

Airmail service may result in faster delivery if the destination is more than 300 miles from the sending office. The time of posting the letters is a key factor in whether airmail service is faster than surface transportation service.

Weather can, of course, be a delaying factor for either kind of service. If roads are blocked for several days by a blizzard, air transportation may be operating sooner than road transportation. On the other hand, surface transportation may be operating no sooner than air transportation if bad weather has closed the airports but not stopped surface travel.

Letters mailed on a Friday by regular mail will usually reach their destinations by Monday unless they are going coast-to-coast.

Special delivery speeds delivery if the recipient is within a radius of one mile of the post office and if the receiving firm does not have a company mail truck picking up mail from the Main Post Office several times a day.

Letters require first-class postage whether they are typewritten, handwritten, carbon copies, or photocopies. Postal rates are based on weight. If the secretary mails letters herself and has a scale for weighing them at the office, she can eliminate the time that might be spent at the stamp counter or the delay because the windows are closed.

34-B. Transcription Craftsmanship

PROOFREADING TECHNIQUES. In proofreading, the transcriber needs to consider three aspects of the skill: fidelity, attractive appearance, and technical correctness.

In proofreading for fidelity, the transcriber must be checking to see whether (a) the dictation has been accurately transcribed, (b) the directions have been followed, (c) the data have been checked for accuracy, (d) the proper service and special notations have been made, and (e) the content makes sense.

In ascertaining whether the dictation had been accurately transcribed, the transcriber would need to check the transcript against her shorthand notes. If she were typing from a typewritten or printed source, she would need to check her copy against that document.

In proofreading for attractive appearance, the transcriber must be examining the transcript for the following desirable characteristics: (a) cleanness of copy, i.e., no unsightly smudges, (b) clearness of print, (c) proper placement on the page, (d) neatness of corrections, (e) proper selection of stationery for the particular

BACKGROUND FOR COMMUNICATION #2. A new business firm is being organized, and a law firm has drawn up the *Articles of Incorporation*, an illustration of which is shown on page iii in the Appendix, for its operation. This dictation includes the first three articles. Other articles deal with such matters as names of the incorporators, how many shares of stock there are to be, the cost of the shares, etc.

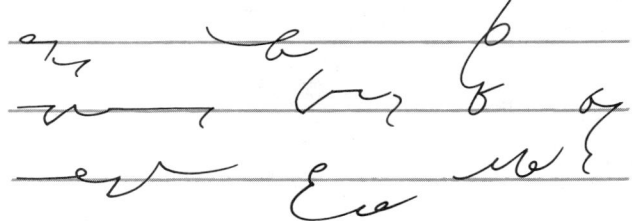

incorporators, lessor, fabricate, instruments, partnerships, suburbs, mercantile, exploit, whatsoever

BACKGROUND FOR COMMUNICATION #3. *The Articles of Incorporation* must be sent to the Secretary of State. The letter of transmittal will be dictated to you.

Lesson 40

transcript being typed. It is assumed, of course, that no secretary would begin transcribing a letter without first making sure that the typewriter keys were clean so that there would be no clogged letters on the final transcript.

In proofreading for technical correctness, the transcriber would need to read the transcript for (a) grammatical correctness, (b) accuracy of spelling, (c) correctness of word division, (d) proper expression of numbers, and (e) correct application of punctuation and capitalization rules.

Proofreading may require more than one examination of the transcript. The material may need to be read first for accuracy of content and sense and read a second time for other aspects.

The transcriber must understand that proofreading is an integral part of transcribing and that she is responsible for proofing.

34-C. Communication in Insurance

BACKGROUND FOR COMMUNICATIONS #1 AND #2. These memos are ones that you practiced in Lesson 33. You will be transcribing from your own notes taken on familiar material.

DIRECTIONS FOR TRANSCRIPTION. Use memo Style 1, illustrated on page i in the Appendix, for your transcripts.

BACKGROUND FOR COMMUNICATION #3. Certain departments in the Home Office have revised the form of the Ordinary Life policy, and this memo is being sent to the field representatives along with a specimen.

34-D. Transcription Capsules

40-C. Executive Language in Law

encumber (en kum′bər), v. 1. to impede or hinder activity; hold back. 2. to burden. 3. to weight down with debts or legal claims.

lessee (les ē′), n. a person who is given a lease.

perpetual (pər pech′ú əl), adj. continuing forever; eternal. 2. lasting throughout life. 3. constant, never ceasing.

40-D. Communication in Law

BACKGROUND FOR COMMUNICATION #1. The executor of O. B. Fisher's estate, Thomas White, has concluded a contest with the Internal Revenue regarding estate taxes due and is writing to Mrs. James to report the final agreement.

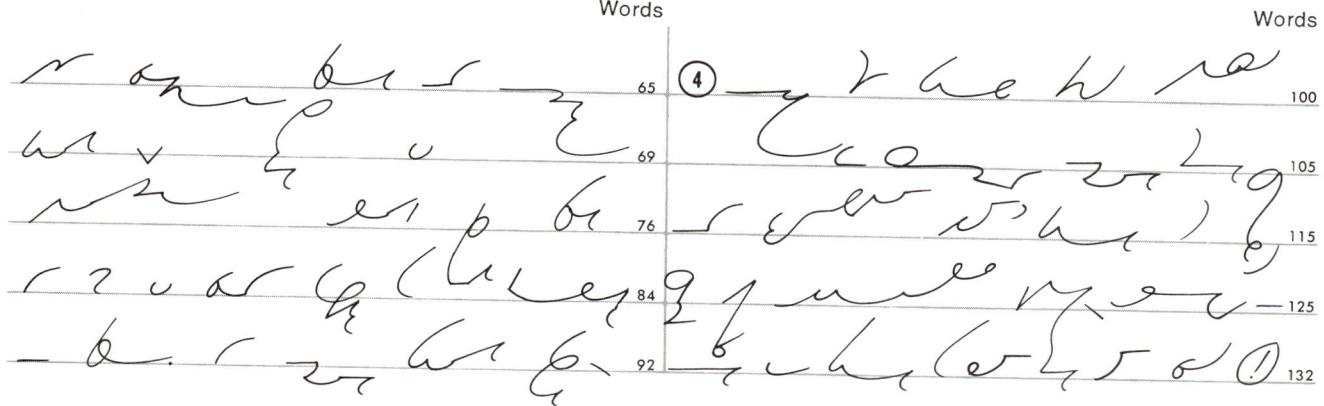

LESSON 35

35-A. System Control

As in Lesson 33, the sentences are of the same dictation length.

35-B. THE OFFICE: A Decision-Making Center

LESSON 40

40-A. System Control

Each take below has 20 standard dictation words.

40-B. THE OFFICE: A Decision-Making Center

35-C. Executive Language in Insurance

sheltered, (shel′ tər d), v. to be covered or protected, as by insurance.

35-D. Communication in Insurance

BACKGROUND FOR COMMUNICATION #1. Mr. Bob Dunn talked with Mr. Irons yesterday and sold him a life insurance plan. Today he is writing a follow-up letter to Mr. Irons expressing his pleasure at having been of service and stating that he will be getting in touch with him as soon as the policy has been prepared.

39-D. Transcription Capsules

BACKGROUND FOR COMMUNICATION #2. The Student Senate has, in cooperation with representatives of insurance companies, formulated a plan for medical insurance to be offered to students. This letter is to the parents of University students to tell them of the policy.

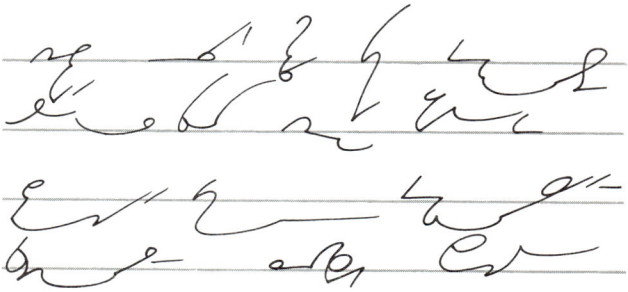

unexpected, medical, upset, budget, consultation, virtually, burden, younger, hospitalization, excluded, supplement, Consolidated, Casualty, enthusiastic, approval

BACKGROUND FOR COMMUNICATION #3. Mr. McCarthy, a representative for Consolidated Casualty Company, is sending a newly purchased annuity contract to Professor Emil T. Lynch. The letter will be dictated in office style.

▶▶▶ LESSON 36 ◀◀◀

36-A. System Control

Each short take consists of 20 standard words, with emphasis on words occurring in the 1,500 most-used words in business correspondence.

UNIT 7 COMMUNICATION IN LAW

The less folding that is used the easier the letter may be opened. For that reason, the folding procedure for the Nos. 7¾, 9, and 10 involves only two folds. The folding procedure for the Nos. 6¾ and 6¼ involves more folds because of the size of the envelope and the sheet to be inserted.

For any size of envelope, the folded letter is inserted into the envelope with the last crease being toward the bottom of the envelope. This procedure is based on the assumption that the letter will be removed by the recipient from the back side of the envelope and, therefore, the recipient can most easily grasp a top corner in opening the missive.

▶ **39-C. Communication in Law**

BACKGROUND FOR COMMUNICATION #1. Dean Gray, attorney at law, notifies Mrs. Peter James that an official survey has been made of property she has sold to the Evans Book Company.

DIRECTIONS FOR TRANSCRIPTION. Display the message in Block format with Open punctuation.

BACKGROUND FOR COMMUNICATION #2. Dean Gray, attorney at law, is informing Mrs. James that a formal offer has been made to purchase a farm that she owns and asks for an indication of whether she wishes to accept.

DIRECTIONS FOR TRANSCRIPTION. Use the same display form as for Communication #2.

36-B. THE OFFICE: A Decision-Making Center

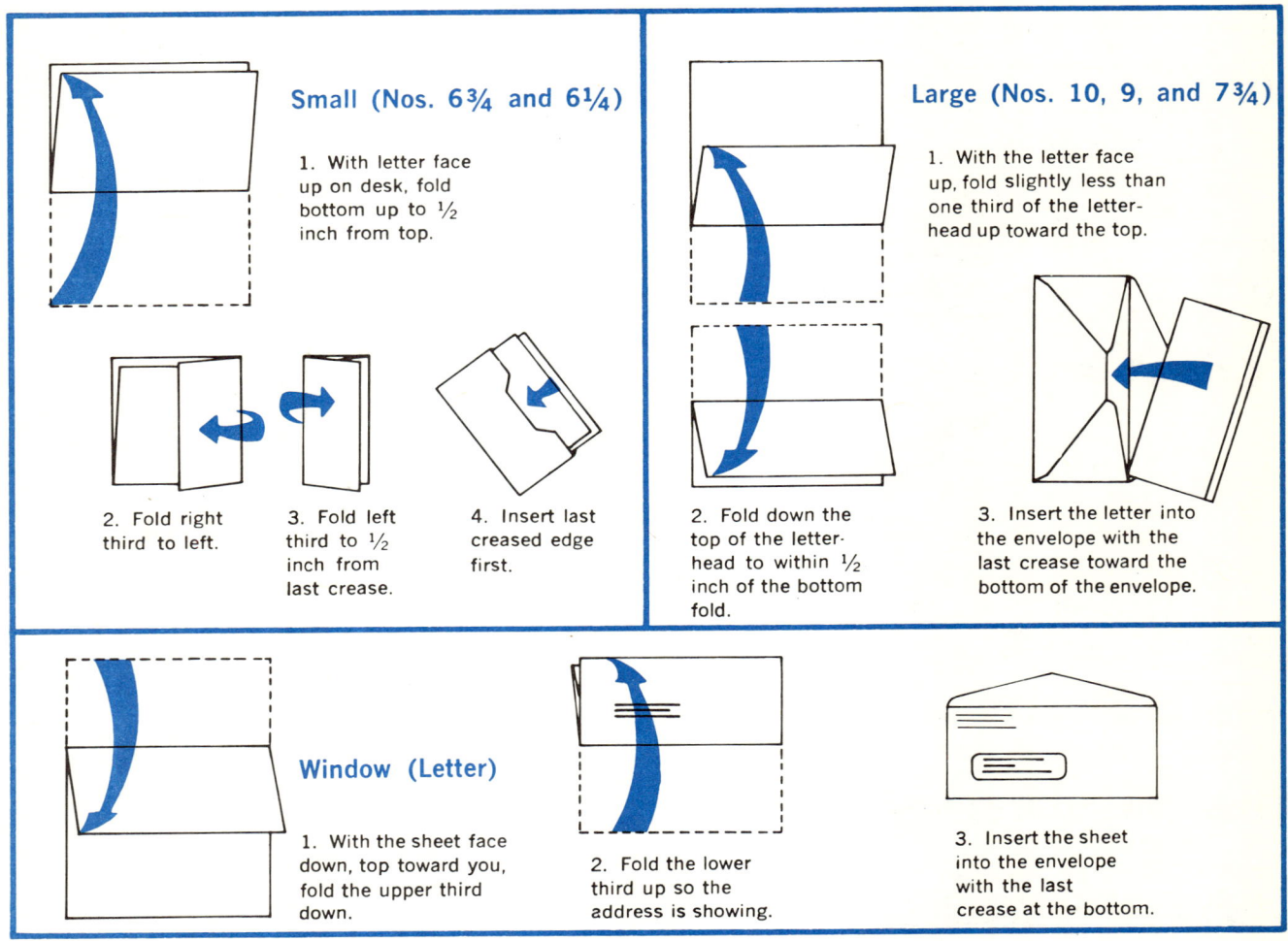

Business Reply envelopes are those enclosed within another envelope; they are already addressed and the postage has already been affixed or guaranteed by the sender, so the person returning his reply has only to insert his message in the Business Reply envelope and mail it. Usually, a Business Reply envelope is slightly smaller than the one in which it is sent. For example, a Business Reply envelope included in an No. 10 envelope might be a No. 9.

If the executive secretary has the responsibility for purchasing stationery, she should be sure that the kind of paper that will be used for the envelopes matches that used for the stationery. Business Reply envelopes, however, may be of lesser quality. She should also investigate the type of glue used on the envelope flaps. In humid climates, some types of glue will cause the flap to stick to the envelope before it is used.

39-B. Transcription Craftsmanship

FOLDING LETTERS FOR INSERTION INTO ENVELOPES. Letters should be folded in such a way as to facilitate their being unfolded by the recipient. A letter opens most easily if the edges of the sheet are not brought exactly together but rather with from ⅓ to ¼ inch from each other as shown in the illustration above.

36-C. Executive Language in Law

adjudge (ə juj'), v. 1. to decide or rule upon. 2. condemn or sentence judicially.

appraise (ə prāz'), v. 1. to estimate the value or amount of. 2. to set a value or price on.

pendency (pen' dən sē), n. the state of being pending.

36-D. Communication in Law

BACKGROUND FOR COMMUNICATION #1. Mr. Fisher has passed away. Mr. Benson, who has been renting a house owned by Mr. Fisher, has bought a home and moved out of the rental property. Mrs. Denhardt, the agent for the estate, has consulted the executor, an attorney, about seeking another renter or selling the house. This letter is his reply.

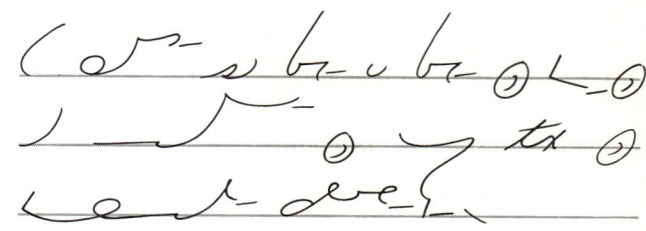

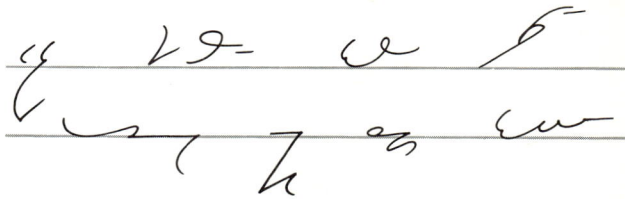

BACKGROUND FOR COMMUNICATION #2. Mr. Woodrow L. Mills makes a sworn statement before the Industrial Accident Board regarding his need for receiving in a lump sum his workmen's compensation for an accident sustained while working for the Dayton Concrete Co.

subscribed, Ft. Wayne, severe, Dayton, lump, injustice, ensue, sworn

BACKGROUND FOR COMMUNICATION #3. A *Narrative Summary* is prepared for submission to the Industrial Accident Board supporting a request for a lump sum settlement.

LESSON 39

39-A. Effective Dispatch of Communications

ENVELOPE SIZES. Sizes of envelopes vary with the sizes of letterhead stationery. The two most commonly used sizes are No. 6¾, which is 6½ by 3⅝ inches, and No. 10, which is 9½ by 4⅛ inches. The smaller size is usually used for one-page letters; the larger size, for letters of more than one page or for letters with enclosures. These two sizes are used for 8½ by 11 stationery. The No. 6¾ is also used for 8½ by 5½ sheets.

The chart shows envelope sizes used for the most commonly used sizes of stationery.

LETTERHEADS			ENVELOPES	
SIZE		NAME	NUMBER	SIZE
8½ x 11		Business or Regular	6¾ / 10	6½ x 3⅝ / 9½ x 4⅛
7¼ x 10½		Executive or Professional	7¾	7½ x 3⅞
8½ x 5½		Half-Sheet	6¾	6½ x 3⅝
8 x 10½		Government	9	8⅞ x 3⅞

BACKGROUND FOR COMMUNICATION #2. Mr. Higgins, the executor for the Fisher estate, is submitting to Mrs. Denhardt a copy of the final account and petition for distribution that he is required by law to submit to the Court. This letter accompanies the document.

petition, commencing, Hunt, Internal Revenue, widow, allowance, rental

BACKGROUND FOR COMMUNICATION #3. A legal document known as an *Order to Show Cause* is dictated. It contains a request that notice be given to the Defendant to appear in Court and answer the application of the Plaintiff regarding temporary custody and support for the children during pendency of a divorce action. The dictation will be office style. An illustration of an *Order to Show Cause* may be found on page ii in the Appendix.

LESSON 37

37-A. Effective Dispatch of Communications

DISTRIBUTION MEDIA FOR EXTERNAL COMMUNICATIONS. Decisions on whether to send a communication by regular mail or airmail need to be made. Is there need for proof of mailing? Is there need to be insured against loss of a document? Special services are available to meet such needs, and the executive secretary must be aware of them.

CERTIFICATE OF MAILING. If proof is needed that a letter or document has been mailed, a certificate of mailing can be purchased. This does not insure or speed delivery; it merely is evidence that an item was mailed.

CERTIFIED MAIL. For a small fee the Post Office will provide a numbered receipt so that the delivery of an item can be traced. The gummed stub of the certified mail receipt is affixed to the envelope; the sender retains the receipt itself, which carries the same number.

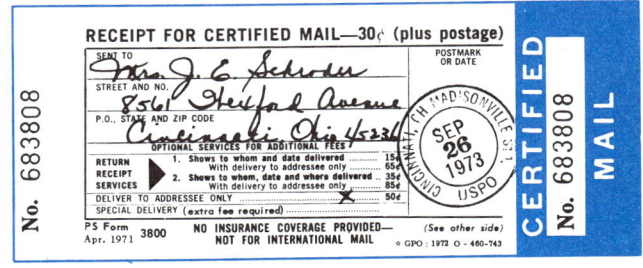

Receipt for Certified Mail

REGISTERED MAIL. A letter or document may be "insured" by registering it at the Post Office. The person doing the mailing fills

Certificate of Mailing

38-C. Executive Language in Law

lawsuit (lô′ süt′), n. a case before a court of law.

manifest (man′ə fest), adj. easily perceived by the senses. v. to make evident by showing. n. ship's list of passengers or cargo.

undersigned (un′ dər sīnd′), adj. having signed at the end of a document. n. person signing a document.

38-D. Communication in Law

BACKGROUND FOR COMMUNICATION #1. Mrs. Martin is not satisfied with the award decided upon by the Industrial Accident Board in her husband's death. Her attorney, Andrew S. Jones, dictates a *Notice of Refusal to Abide by Ruling of Industrial Accident Board*.

in a form which indicates the address of the person who is to receive the letter or document, the sender's address, the nature of the contents, and its value. The envelope must be securely sealed. The sender may obtain a receipt as evidence of delivery by marking the envelope "Return Receipt Requested" and paying an additional fee. If the registered item does not arrive at its destination in a reasonable amount of time, the sender requests the Post Office to trace the item.

AIRMAIL INSURED. If an envelope's contents weighs more than 7 ounces, it can be sent by airmail and insured at a rate less than that required for regular airmail registered fee. The exact fee depends on the weight of the item.

FORWARD MAIL. If the sender wishes the Post Office to forward a letter if the addressee has moved, she should type "Please Forward" on the envelope. If the receiving office wishes to forward a letter that has been received for someone no longer in that office, the original address should be crossed out neatly and the new one written on the envelope. It will be forwarded without additional postage. If the letter had been sent by special delivery, however, the special delivery fee would have to be paid again to have the letter handled by special delivery at the second address.

37-B. Transcription Craftsmanship

ADDRESSING ENVELOPES. The address is usually placed on an envelope in the lower right fourth of the envelope. The reasons are these: (1) Such placement provides for greatest visibility for the postal clerk in sorting. The clerk usually grasps a stack of envelopes with one hand, placing the fingers at the back of the stack for support and the thumb about the center on the top side. The address, then, is likely to be clear for easy reading.

(2) The spacing of addresses on envelopes is also a factor in the ease with which envelopes are sorted. Double-spaced lines are easier to read than single-spaced lines. Therefore, the Post Office suggests double spacing three-line addresses. However, some businesses follow the practice of single spacing all addresses on envelopes as a means of simplifying the operation. For reasons of space, four- and five-line addresses are single spaced.

As the use of the optical scanner equipment increases, uniformity in address style will become desirable. For the machine to "read" addresses correctly, the lines need to be in blocked form.

The address on a No. 6¾ envelope is in excellent position if its first line is on the 13th line from the top edge of the envelope; on a No. 10 envelope, on the 15th line from the top edge.

The illustration below shows good address placement for various sizes of envelopes.

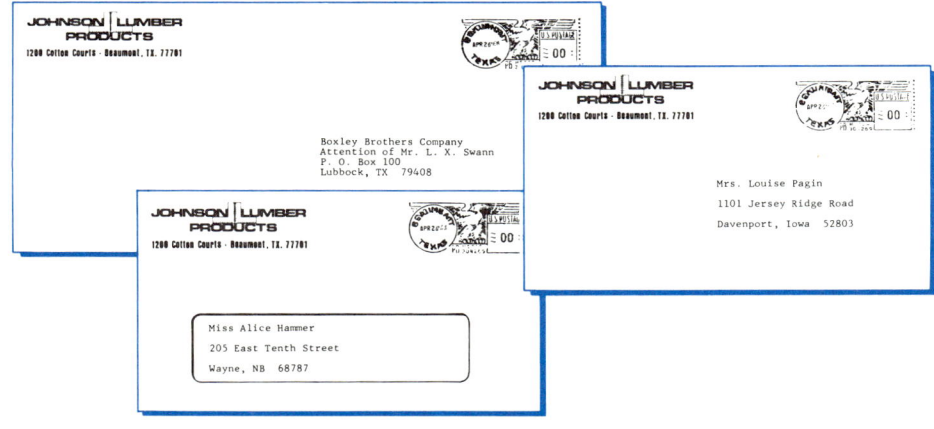

Correctly Addressed Envelopes

LESSON 38

38-A. System Control

The take consists of 20 standard dictation words.

38-B. THE OFFICE: A Decision-Making Center

DISPLAYING MESSAGES IN LETTER FORM. The sender of a letter hopes to effect a favorable response from the person who is to receive the letter. He chooses his words carefully, and he arranges his thoughts so that they are concise and coherent. The message itself must be displayed on the stationery so that it is pleasing to the eye. Display styles take into consideration such factors as letterhead design, space breaks, and signals and codes which are needed.

You are about to begin transcribing letters from your shorthand notes. You must learn to judge the length of a letter from the amount of notes you have taken in your notebook. To help refresh your memory on letter placement factors, a placement guide is illustrated on page iv in the Appendix. Keep in mind the following pointers:

1. Practices vary in the vertical placement of the date line. This table is set up for the use of the *floating* date line, i.e., one whose vertical placement is adjusted to the length of the letter.

2. The setup for a certain length of letter is not always the same. A 100-word letter having a subject line, an attention line, or tabulated material requires a longer writing line than a 100-word letter with none of these factors.

3. The left, right, and bottom margins of a letter on 8½ by 11 stationery should not be less than one inch in width.

4. A letter of fewer than 75 words may be typed with double spacing in the body of the letter.

37-C. Communication in Law

BACKGROUND FOR COMMUNICATION #1. The law firm, Cunningham, Cox, and Cohen, representing Graham Company, is attempting to collect an overdue account. This letter is the last attempt in a series to obtain payment without legal action.

DIRECTIONS FOR TRANSCRIPTION. Transcribe the notes below. Use the display style called Block and the punctuation style called Open. These styles are illustrated on page v in the Appendix. Extraoffice letters require a file copy, just as memos. Address an envelope also.

37-D. ◀ **Transcription Capsules**

BACKGROUND FOR COMMUNICATION #2. Mr. Higgins, the executor for the Fisher estate, is notifying Mrs. Denhardt of the Court hearing for approval of his account and report as executor. When transcribing, use the same display style that you used in Communication #1.

APPENDIX

Memo Style 1 (Lesson 27)

JONES-HARRIS-ADAMS, SECURITIES
Memorandum

```
To      : Dr. Homer D. Gilbert
From    : Ira P. Whittington, Senior Editor
Date    : April 1, 19--
Subject: Illustrative Materials

Excellent illustrative materials add a great deal to the effective-
ness of textual materials.  Through the use of a table, the author
```

Memo Style 2 (Lesson 46)

```
   Date: March 8, 19--
     To: Dr. Fred Thornton, Chief of Staff, Spokane General Hospital
   From: W. A. Leff
Subject: Absence from March 15 to 18

         On March 15 I will leave for the AMA convention in Chicago.
    I will return on the evening of March 18.  My itinerary is
```

Memorandum Report Style (Lesson 68)

```
    TO      : Executive Officers
    FROM    : James F. Cleve, Personnel Officer
    DATE    : June 15, 19--
    SUBJECT : PERSONNEL REPORT FOR THE MONTH OF MAY
                                                   ← triple space
                        Attritions
                                                   ← triple space
Computing Department
                              ← double space
        Key-punch operators.  Of the 18 key-punch operators on duty on
May 1, 1 was dismissed and 2 resigned during the month.

        Computer operators.  Of the 6 computer operators on the payroll
as of May 1, 1 resigned during the month.

        Programmers.  There was no attrition of programmers during the
month of May.
                        ← triple space
Executive Office
        Stenographers.  Of the 12 stenographers on duty on May 1, 2
resigned and 1 requested maternity leave during the month of May.
```

Appendix i

ORDER TO SHOW CAUSE FORM
(Lesson 36)

IN THE UNITED STATES DISTRICT COURT
SOUTHERN DISTRICT OF OHIO
WESTERN DIVISION

JAMES R. DOE   :

   and   :

THE DOE COMPANY   :

   Plaintiffs,   :   CIVIL ACTION

   v.   :   No. 3635

THE XYZ COMPANY   :

   Defendants.   :

ORDER TO SHOW CAUSE

WHEREAS, on the 22nd day of March, 19--, this case came on to be heard on plaintiffs' Motion for a Show Cause Order, was submitted to the Court, and is found to be well taken;

It is therefore, ORDERED, ADJUDGED, AND DECREED, that defendant show cause to the Court why it is entitled to a Protective Order under Rule 26(c)(7) of the Federal Rules; that within twenty days of this Order defendant list those documents heretofore produced for plaintiff which it claims contain confidential or trade secret information accumulated over the years at considerable work and cost and which, if freely disclosed to others, will or may deprive defendant of a competitive advantage in the life insurance industry; that defendant support its claim with legal authority. Within ten days after defendant has listed its documents and stated its legal position, plaintiff shall file its memorandum in opposition to defendant's position.

Appendix ii

ARTICLES OF INCORPORATION
(Lesson 40)

ARTICLES OF INCORPORATION

OF

MIDWAY AIRCRAFT COMPANY, INC.

We, the undersigned, a majority of whom are citizens of the United States, desiring to form a corporation, for profit, under the General Corporation Act of Ohio, do hereby ceritfy:

ARTICLE I. The name of said corporation shall be: Midway Aircraft Company, Inc.

ARTICLE II. The place in Ohio where its principal office is to be located is Cincinnati, Hamilton County.

ARTICLE III. The purpose or purposes for which it is formed are: the manufacture, repair, improvement, and service of aircraft parts.

ARTICLE IV. The maximum number of shares which the corporation is authorized to have outstanding is One Thousand (1,000), all of which shall be with a par value of One Hundred Dollars ($100) each.

A. The corporation shall at all times maintain net current assets at not less than one hundred percent (100%) and total net assets at not less than two hundred percent (200%) of the total par value of the preferred stock then outstanding.

B. The corporation shall not sell or dispose of its entire plant, assets, business or goodwill or any real estate, without the affirmative vote or written consent of the holders of seventy-five percent (75%) or more of the preferred stock at the time outstanding.

ARTICLE V. The amount of capital with which the corporation will begin is Two Hundred Thousand Dollars ($200,000).

In witness whereof, we have hereunto subscribed our names, this Fifth day of March, 19--.

_____.
_____.
_____.

The State of Ohio, County of Hamilton, ss.
 Personally appeared before me, the undersigned a Notary Public, in and for said county, this Fifth day of March, 19--, the above named Glen Hughes, LeRoy Cason, and John Schroder, who each severally acknowledged the signing of the foregoing articles of incorporation to be his free act and deed, for the uses and purposes therein mentioned.
 Witness my hand and official seal on the day and year last aforesaid.

_____, Notary Public.

LETTER PLACEMENT TABLE
(Lesson 37)

Letter Placement Table [1]

Letter Classification		5-Stroke Words in Letter Body	Side Margins	Date Line Position [2] (From Top Edge of Paper)
Short		Up to 100	2″	Line 20
Average	1	101 - 150	1½″	18
	2	151 - 200	1½″	16
	3	201 - 250	1½″	14
	4	251 - 300	1½″	12
Long		301 - 350	1″	12
Two-page		More than 350	1″	12

[1] The assumption has been made that the letter will have three lines in the inside address and will have closing lines consisting of: complimentary close, company name, and dictator's name or title. If the letter being transcribed has more lines in the inside address, more lines in the closing, or fewer lines in the closing, adjustment in the placement of the letter is made by altering the position of the date line or the margin width or both.

[2] Vertical placement of the date varies according to letter length. The address, however, is typed on the 4th line (3 blank line spaces) below the date. Also, when a deep letterhead makes it impossible to type the date on the designated line, type it a double space below the last letterhead line.

HEADINGS FOR MULTIPAGE LETTERS
(Lesson 55)

```
Mr. J. L. Bly              2              May 9, 19--
                    (triple space)
    so that we can make our plans accordingly.  It may well feature
```

Horizontal Style

```
    Conrad Corporation
    Page 2
    March 15, 19--
                    (triple space)
    by April 10.  Please be sure to include the names of all company
```

Block Style

MESSAGE AND REPLY FORM
(Lesson 63)

```
TO: Dave Brown          FROM: John Thomas
    Production Manager         Purchasing Agent


    SUBJECT: Model C100 Tool Cutter

DATE May 5, 19--          MESSAGE
    The Model C100 Tool Cutter is no
    longer manufactured.  Perhaps
    Model A-1, described on page 410
    of the Acme Catalog will be
    satisfactory, even though it has
    a slightly larger cutting edge.
    If so, we shall order it for you.

    Please let us know if you wish the
    Model A-1 ordered.     John Thomas
             SIGNED

DATE            REPLY




                SIGNED
```

Original (sent to addressee then returned to sender)

First Copy (retained by addressee)

Last Copy (retained by sender)

Appendix iv

LETTER DISPLAY STYLES

**Block Style
with
Open Punctuation
(Lesson 37)**

**Modified Block Style
with Indented Paragraphs,
Mixed Punctuation,
and Centered Date
(Lesson 41)**

**Modified Block Style
with Open Punctuation,
Blocked Paragraphs,
and Centered Date
(Lesson 50)**

Appendix v

ITINERARY
(Lesson 46)

```
                  ITINERARY FOR ERIC H. ROGERS
                        March 16-23, 19--

Monday, March 16:

     4:00 p.m. (EDT.)   Leave office for Cleveland-Hopkins Airport.

     5:00 p.m. (EDT)    Leave Cleveland on United Airlines #425.
                        (Ticket in United Airlines envelope in
                        trip folder.)  Snacks served in flight.

     6:21 p.m. (EDT)    Arrive New York, LaGuardia Airport.
                        Limousine to East Side Terminal at 37th
                        Street and First Avenue.
                        Taxicab to the New York Hilton Hotel at
                        Rockefeller Center.  (Confirmation of
                        hotel reservation in trip folder.)

     7:34 p.m. (EDT)    Convention registration and hospitality
                        hour.  (Empire Room--second floor of the
                        Hilton.)

Tuesday, March 17:

     All day            Convention meetings including banquet.
                        (Convention program with tickets for the
                        March 17 banquet in envelope marked
                        "Convention" in trip folder.)

                        Reminder:  Try to meet Donald S. Hay, Editor
                                              Golf International
                                              Paramus, New Jersey

Wednesday, March 18:

     Morning            Convention meetings including luncheon.
       and              (Ticket for March 18 luncheon in
     Afternoon          "Convention" envelope.)
```

NEWS RELEASE
(Lesson 60)

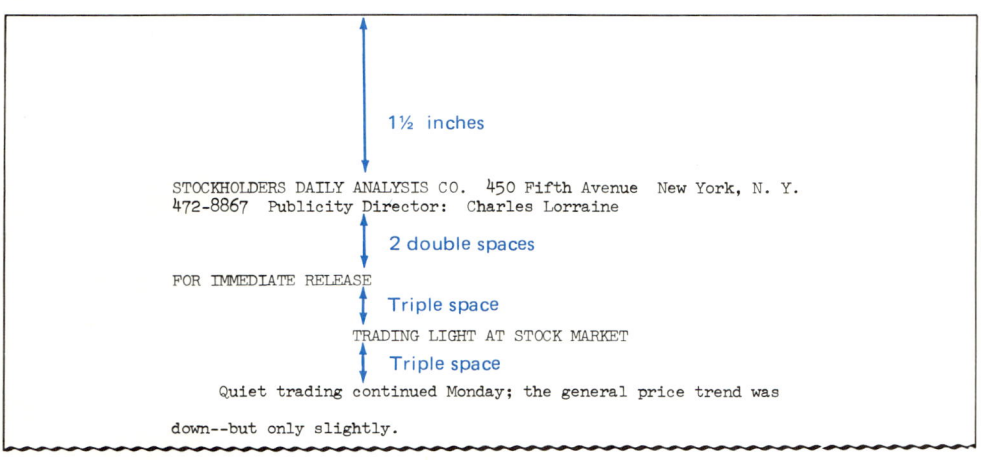

SPECIAL LETTER STYLES

AMS Simplified Letter Style
(Lesson 53)

Official or Informal Letter Style
with Centered Date
and Indented Paragraphs
(Lesson 56)

Government Letter Style
with Date Ending
at Right Margin
(Lesson 58)

Appendix vii

25 PUNCTUATION RULES

Rule 1. Use a comma to set off a dependent caluse that precedes a main clause.

Rule 2. Use a comma to separate coordinate clauses joined by one of the pure conjunctions unless the clauses are very short.

Rule 3. Definite numbers over ten are written in figures. Numbers from one to ten inclusive are written as words. Always spell out a number that begins a sentence. Amounts of money and percentages are expressed in figures whether they are above or below ten and whether they are definite or approximate. Even amounts of money are written without the decimal and ciphers; amounts below $1 are written as a figure and are followed by the word "cent" or "cents" as appropriate.

Rule 4. Use a semicolon between coordinate clauses that are joined by a pure conjunction when either or both of the clauses contain a comma.

Rule 5. In a compound sentence, use a semicolon between clauses that are joined by a conjunctive adverb, such as **so, therefore, hence, yet, however, otherwise, still,** and **furthermore.** (50-D-1)

Rule 6. Use a comma to separate words, phrases, or clauses in a series.

Rule 7. Use a comma to separate a nonrestrictive phrase or clause from the rest of the sentence. Restrictive phrases or clauses are not separated from the rest of the sentence because they are essential to the meaning of the sentence.

Rule 8. Use a comma to set off parenthetical expressions if a definite pause is indicated.

Rule 9. Capitalize the first word and all important words in titles of books, periodicals, and articles. Titles of books, booklets, magazines, and newspapers may be typed entirely in capitals, or they may be underlined with only the first word and all important words capitalized.

Rule 10. Use commas to set off words of direct address.

Rule 11. Use a comma to set off words in apposition.

Rule 12. Use a comma to set off an introductory adverbial phrase containing a verb. Use a comma to set off an introductory phrase that does not contain a verb if a pause would be made at that point in reading or if a comma at that point is essential for emphasis or clarity.

Rule 13. Use a comma to separate from the main clause a clause of reason introduced by **for** or **as** and a clause of concession introduced by **though** or **although.**

Rule 14. Use a comma to set off an introductory participial phrase.

Rule 15. Use a comma to separate two consecutive parallel adjectives modifying a single noun.

Rule 16. Use a comma to set off a phrase denoting residence when it is used with the name of a person. Use a comma to separate the parts of addresses, dates, and geographical names.

Rule 17. Hyphenate a compound adjective if used before a noun.

Rule 18. Spell out names of states unless accompanied by cities. Do not abbreviate such titles as Governor, Professor, etc., when they precede only the last names of persons. An abbreviation may be written without punctuation when used as a symbol for the name of an organization. Spell out units of measure, unless they occur frequently, such as in tabulations or invoices.

Rule 19. Use a comma to precede **for instance, namely, viz, i.e.,** and **that is.** These words may be preceded by a semicolon, a colon, or a dash if they precede an enumeration of several items.

Rule 20. Spell out street names that are numbers up to twelve. State house numbers in figures except for house number One. If a street number follows a house number, it is sometimes written 181 - 15 Street or 181 Fifteenth Street.

Rule 21. Use a dash to indicate a sudden change in the structure of a sentence.

Rule 22. Use quotation marks to enclose each direct quotation.

Rule 23. Use a colon after an introductory expression to indicate that a listing or explanation follows.

Rule 24. Use a comma to indicate the omission of words necessary for the completeness of a sentence.

Rule 25. A semicolon is used between clauses of a compound sentence that are not joined by a conjunction.

PROOFREADERS' MARKS

MARK	EXPLANATION	MARK	EXPLANATION
⊙	Period	*Cap.* e̲ east	Capitalize or all caps
⋀	Comma	*lc.* ᵗTell	Lower case
⊙	Semicolon	⌒	Close up entirely; take out space
⊙	Colon	ℓ	Delete, take out
?/	Question mark	ℓ	Delete and close up
=/	Hyphen	#	Insert space (or more space)
⋁	Apostrophe	⋀	Insert letter or word
(/)	Parentheses	enclosed	Transpose matter in ring
[	Move to left	∩	Transpose letters in a word
]	Move to right	effect affect	Strike out and substitute
¶	Start new paragraph	stet seven	Disregard previous correction

Appendix viii

WITHDRAWN